PRAISE FOR *Chopsticks and Chocolate*

Betty reviewed an early draft of Edward's story in 2006; here are excerpts of her comments (it took 15 years for God to answer her prayer). I was in her women's Bible study and a retreat in the UP of Michigan:

"Being a believer myself and loving both history and geography, it was a real page-turner for me in many ways … where would he go next and what would he find? … what would he do and what would be the outcome? ... God's grace is amazing that brought Edward to America in the first place … It is unbelievable that Edward was able to meet the challenges that he faced and the level of hard work that he maintained. The harm of racial discrimination was heart-breaking.

The recording of both Edward and Monika's coming to Christ was meaningful to me.

Edward, blessings on you for your commitment to honor the Lord and be so transparent about your own life. It is my prayer that the Lord will bring much joy to you as you see this book published. What a wonder to know that the Lord has "restored to you the years that the locusts have eaten" (Joel 2:25) … and is using you to help so many untold people who will take your story to heart … and find salvation, not only for their gambling addiction but in the Lord who is not willing that any should perish.

Betty Lou King, Southfield MI
Faithful Bible teacher to countless students and women for over five decades.
She died at 92 in September 2018. and is gratefully remembered
by Monika and her son Arnold

***

Chopsticks and Chocolate:

This book is an inspiring and intimate look into the life and times of a remarkable couple, Monika and Edward Lumsdaine. Their story is a chronicle of the events that occurred along the way toward their goal of living the American Dream. From a middle-class family in Switzerland and a slum boyhood in Shanghai these two somehow met in Ventura California and their amazing journey together commenced. Sometimes things just seemed to fall in place, but it wasn't always easy. Their future was ultimately earned by their own strength of character, hard work, integrity and perseverance. Yes, the story is compelling by itself and in a real sense a love story. But it's more than that.

Most of us living in America have enjoyed a life of abundance. This has made it easy to overlook the existence of God. We can now believe in our own "self-sufficiency". A story like this makes that existence of God impossible to intellectually or spiritually ignore. Were all of the significant things that helped make Monika and Edward's life so remarkable just coincidental? That's not so. The loving hand of God was with this couple throughout their lives even before they knew it. Every American should read this book.

Jim Arber
Journalist, US Navy, Analytical/Technical Writer, GM
Other writing adventures

***

I met Jim while we were both working in the community garden; when he heard about the book, he said he would love to review it, being a writer himself. The next four reviewers are members of the Saints Alive class at Cedar Springs Presbyterian Church, Knoxville, TN (due to the pandemic, we have not yet met Tom in person, but he was recommended by one of our pastors).

East meets west in this unlikely love story of two people who were pursuing the American Dream. Their love for learning draws them from China (Chopsticks) & Switzerland (Chocolate) to Ventura, California. We get a glimpse of the unseen hand of God orchestrating their lives throughout the book using individuals to help navigate their lives in a new culture.

Their deep love for each other & commitment to God triumphs. It encourages the reader to trust God's overarching plan for each individual through the twists & turns of everyday life.

Albert Ebenezer, MD
Retired Oncologist, Knoxville TN

***

This is a delightful story of two people from opposite geography, culture and races, coming together to love and live. It is a record of hard work, gifted intelligence, and the advantages of life in a free country. As one reads this, it could be assumed that reaching the pinnacle of human achievement would result in ultimate happiness and fulfillment. Edward and Monika discovered what Blaise Pascal pointed out that "There is a God shaped vacuum in the heart of every man which cannot be filled by any created thing, but only by God." This Creator God chose, redeemed and filled that vacuum, so that the two became truly one, with a life dedicated to glorifying and serving the God who saved them. This book would be especially helpful to students and young professionals, who have been stirred to wonder if human education, intellect and effort can really fill the existing vacuum.

Tom Musselman
Pastor, Evangelist
Master of Divinity Chaplain, Colonel U.S. Army Retired

***

This book, *Chopsticks and Chocolate*, shows us a life-long faithful journey of a biracial and bicultural couple under God's hands. This book will challenge readers through the couple's personal struggles, spiritual growth, and restorations as they adjust to each other's background while living in an unfamiliar country, America.

Edward and Monika's testimonies let young adults especially learn how God's enduring love holds each of His people, and He always watches over His people and never gives up. Even though some painful memories from Edward's childhood influenced how he formed relationships with God and his immediate family, God turned these difficulties into a new perspective that let Edward see opportunities and people who need help in this foreign country. How Monika endures and grows, keeping up with being a mother of four, will echo in young readers' hearts who are living in the dark with patience and indefinite hope in their career, relationships, and marriage. The two of us in our journey as a young Christian couple hope to be on a life-long quest in the way Edward and Monika have been walking with Jesus as the only secure foundation of their faith and are still walking forward.

Jun Lee & Joanne Bong
Originally from South Korea, the couple came to America to study in 2012.
Jun is now a post-doc researcher at Oak Ridge National Laboratory;
Joanne seeks a Master's degree in music composition from UT.

Chopsticks and Chocolate

A Love Story Bridging Time and Cultures

Edward Lumsdaine

and

Monika Lumsdaine

Published by KHARIS PUBLISHING, imprint of KHARIS MEDIA LLC.

ISBN-13: 978-1-63746-078-8

ISBN-10: 1-63746-078-3

Library of Congress Control Number: 2021948190

Photo of Mission San Buenaventura: www.pinterest.com; https://s-media-cache-ak).pinimg.com (Dan Dapia), downloaded 5/15/2016; then cropped and enhanced.

Family photos are from Edward and Monika Lumsdaine's family albums, unless otherwise noted.

All KHARIS PUBLISHING products are available at special quantity discounts for bulk purchase for sales promotions, premiums, fund-raising, and educational needs. For details, contact:

Kharis Media LLC
Tel: 1-479-599-8657
support@kharispublishing.com
www.kharispublishing.com

For our precious grandchildren,
lest they forget from where they have come.

All the days ordained for me were written in your book
before one of them came to be.
How precious to me are your thoughts, O God!
Psalm 139:16-17

And now these three remain: faith, hope and love.
But the greatest of these is love.
1 Corinthians 13:13

Contents

Foreword

This memoir is different—it is not strictly a chronological sequel to the story of Edward Lumsdaine's youth as told in *Rotten Gambler Two Becomes a True American: A Boy's Journey of Surviving the Odds* (2016). Many readers of his adventures wanted to know what happened next. Our daughter suggested that the framework should be her parents' love story. Both of us struggled to adjust to each other's cultural background, as well as living in an unfamiliar country. Now, when we look back eight decades, we are astonished to recognize how God worked behind the scenes in our lives, brought us together, and blessed us beyond anything we could ever expect, imagine, or deserve.

In the title, chopsticks are a tool for eating properly, whereas chocolate is special for imparting flavor and sweetness to food. Together, they are a metaphor for the two crucial aspects of love, in *doing* and in *being*. Chopsticks originated in ancient China. In contrast, the smooth Swiss chocolate was developed through innovation by many entrepreneurs over the last two centuries.

A love story bridging time and culture? The story didn't start with our first meeting. We needed to go back to our parents, because they influenced how we experienced (or did not experience) love. But what do we mean by culture? After much discussion, we have come up with three main ways of looking at culture for the benefit of our story.

1. *Culture as a particular way of life of a group of people.* Edward grew up in the context of the Chinese urban culture mainly during wartime. Even though he left China at age 14, it still affects his value system, especially through the influence of his mother who stressed education and following the rules, but was conflicted about gambling. Similarly, Monika having grown up in a small Swiss town has a value system of order and thrift conveyed by her father. Thus, reconciling the cultures of our origins was the first bridge we had to build when we fell in love and wanted a strong marriage.

2. *American culture in the 1960s.* Early in our marriage, both of us had to adjust to a culture focused on freedom, as well as personal growth and development. We encountered local cultures and racial prejudices, the

latter fortunately changing significantly for the better over the decades since then. Edward was much more sensitive to racial prejudice, whereas Monika barely noticed. He was to find prejudice in different forms throughout his entire life, including in universities where he least expected it.

3. *Personal cultures and beliefs.* Simultaneously, our personal development and beliefs grew in different directions, separating us and requiring great effort to bridge. Edward had an almost single-minded focus on work and being financially successful. Monika's faith and dependence on Jesus Christ as her Savior was tested during the years of Edward's struggle to overcome gambling addiction, until our merciful God bridged the gap and strengthened our love.

These different, and sometimes conflicting, cultures are the underlying context of the ups and downs of our love story, the way we raised our family, and in the end how we adjusted to retirement and found contentment.

In addition, there was another concept—The American Dream—that led us to want to become a part of this country. We are now wondering if the many illegal immigrants today, especially the voices clamoring for socialism, really understand what is meant by this concept.

Based on research, we found that the American Dream is the notion that there should be protection for each person's own idea of pursuing happiness (from *The Declaration of Independence*). In 1931, historian James Trudow Adams wrote the following definition in his book, *The Epic of America:* "The American Dream is that dream of a land in which life should be better and richer and fuller for everyone, with opportunity for each according to ability or achievement, … with social order and regardless of circumstance of birth or position."

The inspiring idea from the Founding Fathers will continue to evolve. Both the right to pursue happiness and the right to disagree about what it means are what makes the American Dream so powerful. A free-market economy is seen as a central key, as are home ownership and education, in the path to achieving the American Dream. In other words, it is the belief that anyone, regardless of origin (race or country), class, or the right connections, can attain success in a society where upward mobility is possible for everyone, because it is achieved through vision, hard work, and faith! We both came from more confining cultures, so this Dream was a common goal for us.

We struggled for years to finish writing our love story. We finally realized we had two timespans, the first one covering our youth, our marriage, our college education, and the birth of our four children. The second time span is condensed into a Postscript that summarizes raising our children, our professional lives, and the battles with addiction that end with God's redemption and renewal.

The cultural changes between the early years of our story and the present are striking. Although we want what we have learned about God's intervention in our lives to be a blessing for our grandchildren and perhaps future generations, we envision our book being a source of inspiration for a wider audience, especially of young adults seeking direction in their lives!

PART ONE

Growing-Up Years
1932-1958

10 June 2020

My dear Grandchildren:

The first part of this book provides a glimpse of the events that shaped your grandmother and me until the time we met. It is amazing that we would end up in the same place at the same time, having grown up on opposite sides of the world. And the year 1932 turned out to be significant in the lives of both of our parents.

The first chapter of this book gives you the briefest of summaries about my life, until my honorable discharge from the US Air Force in California, where I started junior college. I describe in more detail my relationship with my parents and the threads that had the strongest influence on me. You will see photos not included in my first book.

Chapters 2 through 4 tell the story of how your grandmother grew up and came to America, with Chapters 5 and 6 describing our first semester in college—stories you may want to pass on to your future families, since such incredible changes have occurred over the course of our lives and in American culture.

With much love from Yehyeh (your "paternal grandfather" in Cantonese).

CHAPTER ONE

Edward: Threads from the Past

When my American father met my mother on a blind date in the lobby of the Cathay Hotel in Shanghai in August of 1932, did it enter their minds or hearts what would be set into motion? Could they imagine having eleven children and that my mother (being Chinese) would call her second son "rotten gambler two"? What mattered was that my mother broke the taboo against marrying a "white ghost" (as the Chinese referred to Caucasians)—a cultural norm starting to crumble in cosmopolitan Shanghai at that time. Being biracial would be something I struggled with all my life. I did not learn that among my father's ancestry were English and Scottish kings (see Appendix 1) until years later, though it made no difference.

Through the years of Japanese occupation, the Communist takeover, and the many incidents that I barely survived against all odds, I developed a deep longing for the American Dream. But what I was able to achieve turned out to be quite different from what I expected. I did find a treasure, but almost lost it, when I fell from a pinnacle of professional achievement through careless and then compulsive gambling. Thus, our story is about a life-long quest, of God's providence and redemption, and of enduring love.

My strongest memory of living in Shanghai is being hungry. There was never enough to eat. My mother would cook a pot of rice for our supper, and occasionally we had a bit of fish and vegetables. Enough rice was then left at the bottom of the pot to be covered with water and boiled into congee for our breakfast the next day. I had sores between my fingers from lack of vitamins. This was during the time when the Japanese occupied the International Settlement in Shanghai where we lived.

Whenever he went out, my father, as an American, had to wear an armband with an "A" on it. This would have been shortly after Pearl Harbor in December 1941. I have a vague recollection of my mother and grandmother talking about the fact that people in the other concessions in Shanghai had to wear armbands, too, such as a "B" for Britain and "N" for the Netherlands. In February 1943, the Japanese arrested my father and imprisoned him in a concentration camp, because he was an American. My

Cantonese mother and their biracial children were allowed to continue living in a tenement apartment with her mother, the orphaned niece, and two servants.

Air raid sirens. Darkness, since all windows were blacked out and lights off. Curfew. Sneaking out with my older brother Chuck to snitch food from the market which had been left unattended because the vendors were ordered to seek shelter during air raids. Beaten for grabbing slices of radish set out to dry by my mother on our roof top. All of us were hungry!

At times we received a large food box provided by the US government through the Swiss Red Cross (minus the vitamins confiscated by the Japanese soldiers). It took a while to get used to sauerkraut and canned cheese, which my mother viewed with great suspicion.

By 1944, we did not know if our father was still alive. When Japan surrendered at the end of World War II, I was almost eight years old. My mother and grandmother were overjoyed that the Imperial Army had been defeated—several family members had been killed by them. But what was going to happen to us now? Then my emaciated father returned on 26 August 1945. Although I knew he was a white man, I was surprised—I rarely saw a "white ghost." I had not remembered what he looked like, not having seen him but once in almost three years. My older brother and sister later told me that he was a changed man. He hardly ever spoke about the time he was interned. I only remember him saying that his Australian bunk mate was shot in front of all the prisoners as an example when the guards discovered that he listened to "The Voice of America" on a hidden radio. My mother was concerned about his being depressed for years. Today, this would be recognized as a symptom of post-traumatic stress disorder.

During the next turbulent years, my father had a job with American President Lines. After the Communists took over Shanghai in 1949, he started to have nightmares. He would stand by the barred windows, trembling and calling out in mixed Mandarin and Cantonese, "They are coming for me!" Then he lost his job, after his company closed due to lack of business. Our parents decided that my father should return to the US where he could draw his back pay and find a good job.

He and Chuck did get a discounted fare on the *President Wilson* to San Francisco. It would be nearly ten years before the family was reunited in

California. During the McCarthy era, my father found it impossible to land a good-paying job, due to his lack of education and his biracial family. He did not have the prestige he had enjoyed in Shanghai, and he worried how mom and the children would adjust to this climate of racial prejudice.

My Relationship with My Father

I experienced my father as distant and aloof. I only remember two direct interactions with him. Once, I got spanked unjustly for having turned on the radio to listen to some semi-classical music. My brother, Chuck, was the culprit. The other I treasure: it is the memory of a rare gift, a ruler, placed under my pillow one Christmas. I recall with sadness that it was only on his deathbed that he held my hand. There were no hugs, ever, in the Chinese culture which he had adopted. I would later be grateful when he came with me to the US Air Force recruiting station in San Francisco on my seventeenth birthday, to sign his permission for me to join the military. I was not living with him at the time, and it would be years before I saw him again.

The legacy he left for me is being a man scrupulously honest despite difficult circumstances, and working hard at whatever menial jobs he was able to get in America after his years in China. Like him, I have found it difficult all my life to open up and share my deepest feelings with my family, even though I deeply love my wife, my four children, and my grandchildren.

These early experiences of surviving in a city occupied in turn by the Japanese, the Nationalist soldiers, and then the Communists, with mostly an absentee father, resulted in three strong goals: I wanted an *excellent education* for myself (and later for my children), which would lead to good jobs to provide *food* on the table and a secure *roof* over our heads, for which I made up the acronym FREE. This eventually turned into a long-lasting and consuming compulsion. Although my relationship with my father remained distant his entire life, there is something else I think I inherited from him and his ancestors: being broadminded toward people from different cultures, countries and backgrounds, and a willingness for travel and moving to new places when getting bored with the same old routines at work.

My Father's Upbringing

Looking back at my father's childhood, I recognize that he did not have what we consider to be a good role model for fatherhood himself. Clifford Vere Lumsdaine was born in Seattle and weighed only four pounds. His mother, Nellie Clifford (see photo), whose family had emigrated from Ireland to Iowa, died of diabetes when he was two years old. His father remarried and Clifford grew up for a while with a half-brother, Arthur. I fondly remember him as my Uncle Art.

In interviews with family members, my father mentioned the following details about his early life:

I remember living in Juneau, Alaska, then San Francisco, and then traveling by ship in 1918 to Australia. We were all sick with the pandemic influenza and were quarantined until everyone on board had recovered. I lived with my grandparents for some time. They called me "the kid" (which I liked). Then it was felt I should be with younger people; thus, I was sent to live with Uncle Allan and Aunt Kate for a while. I loved my grandparents who were very religious, and I was helping with raising chickens and vegetables. I returned to San Francisco in 1926 where I went to high school and worked as a stock clerk for a wholesale druggist.

Then from November 1929 to January 1930 I was a messman on the SS Oregonian, *sailing a San Francisco to New York round trip. Next, I worked for the Southern Pacific Steamer division from May 1928 to November 1929. When my father asked me to join him in Shanghai to help with his business, I did so from January 1930 to June 1933. This was the Lumsdaine Oriental Company (import and export), until it went out of business. During that time, I first lived with his new wife and two children (Virginia and Jack), then moved to the YMCA.*

Virginia, my father's stepsister, was a British subject and was also interned by the Japanese during World War II. Her experiences of growing up in Shanghai are depicted in an award-winning documentary, *My Shanghai, a True Story of Love, War, and Other Seasons*, by P.H. Wells, First Straw Films.

My father did not like us to disparage or joke about his father, even though he had married twice without benefit of divorce from Arthur's mother. I still don't understand why my father never mentioned he had worked on a ship as a messman. I had a similar experience as a messman covering the same route from California to New York, but then traveled very much further across the Pacific Ocean to the Far East as far as Thailand, the Philippine Islands, and Japan.

What Started in 1932

In the two paragraphs below, my youngest sister Dolly describes the marriage of our parents. Our youngest brother Albert was to call them "indomitable" in a 2020 biography (see the bottom of the following page).

Mom and Dad clearly had a very unconventional marriage and life. I have often reflected on what it must have been like for them, a young white man and a young Chinese woman as lovers in the early 1930s—what they must have encountered. Shanghai then was a hotbed of young people overturning all kinds of age-old (feudal) traditions, and apparently Mom was part of her generation's thumbing their noses at their parents, like women cutting their braids and wearing short hair, daring to go to a darkened movie theater and sit next to men, even wearing white tennis shoes (challenging the superstitious belief of bad luck since white is the color of mourning in China). They had to defy "the way things are" out of the love they had for each other, to have gone against friends, family and the general public's disapproval.

Admirable was Dad's daring to tackle a most difficult thing by thoroughly adopting the Chinese culture—learning the language (Mom didn't see the need to learn English). Some of the most interesting stories my parents told me were about their wildly romantic courtship: Mom taking the gun away from her previous Chinese boyfriend when he threatened to shoot Dad for winning Mom's heart, or Mom going as far as fist fights with Shanghai cabbies daring to bad-mouth their interracial relationship to her face.

Theirs was a bond held firmly together by the most genuine love, since Dad never had fame nor fortune to offer Mom as a security deposit. Obviously, they both had and further developed a proud, willful attitude and character to get them through tough times.

The photo of my parents as a young couple (circa 1932) shows Choi Yuk-Cheun and Choi Ho Wei-Ying (my mother's sister and husband) on the left. with Clifford Vere Lumsdaine and Ho Miao Ying. She grew up in the Shunde district of Foshan City, about 30 miles south of Guangzhou (jCanton) until 1928). Neither parent approved of their dating and engagement. Mom's father Ho Kok Peh disinherited her, and Dad's father stopped speaking to him. When the business failed in 1933, his father left for Australia, leaving Dad to cope with the creditors. To escape death threats by angry creditors, Dad uprooted his family by moving to Hong Kong.

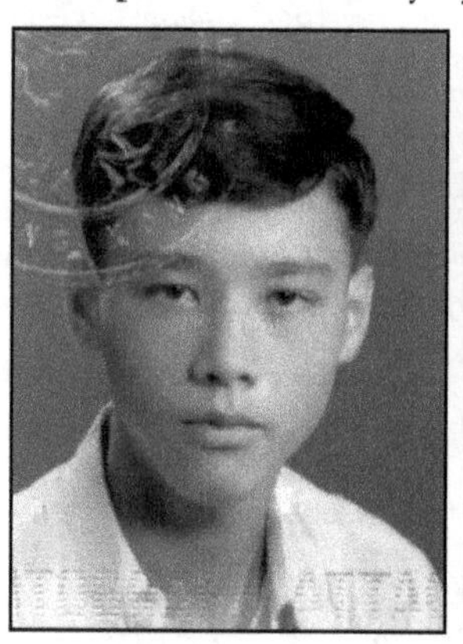

Recently I saw a photo of my maternal grandfather and was struck at how much I resemble him in my lower face shown on my passport photo at age 14 (in the photos above). And I inherited my maternal grandmother Liang Yee Dai's eyes! Their photos are from my youngest brother, who wrote, over the last four years, a book about our parents, *INDOMITABLE, a Legacy of Love, Courge and Perseverance, ©2020 Joseph Albert Lumsdaine.The book is available on amazon.com*

My parents were united by a Buddhist priest in a marriage contract in Hong Kong, before their first son, Charles, was born. In 1935, Dad got a job as a secretary with Paramount. When the job was terminated in 1939, he decided to return to Shanghai, where Mom's parents and sister still lived. Despite the threat of war and dangers of this travel, Mom's brother and family also wanted to move to Shanghai. The separate ship that they took was torpedoed by the Japanese, with everyone in the family lost, except one male cousin who proved to be a good swimmer and one female cousin, Ho Siu Hwa, who had traveled with our family to help with the babies. The rail line having been cut, the only choice was to go by sea.

Then in 1940, right after Mom's father had died, the couple were "officially" married in a western-style ceremony on Friday, September 27, at the American Consulate in Shanghai. This ensured that their four living children (Chuck, Maria, Edward, and George) would have US citizenship. From then on, Grandmother lived with us, as did the orphaned cousin Ho Siu Hwa.

Male Figures "in Loco Parentis"

I want to mention some of the fatherly attention I received from other male figures during my growing-up years. Firstly, my Uncle Choi Yuk-Cheun stood up for me, proclaiming to the rest of the family that I would have a great future. When I was expelled from St. Joan of Arc Catholic School by the headmaster, Brother Gilbert, "for fighting, playing hooky and being a bad influence on another student," Uncle arranged a place for me at the St. Xavier Catholic School, in the neighborhood where he lived. And I've always appreciated a wonderful gift he gave me—a watch, even though I had to sell it in my attempts to get enough money to make it to Hong Kong.

By 1952, I was desperate to leave Shanghai and find my own way to San Francisco. Not only did I not fit into the Chinese culture, being biracial, but anti-American feelings ran high in China because of the Korean War. I sold everything I had and boldly borrowed the train fare from Father Peter, a priest at the Church of Christ the King. He did not know me, but his kindness made a deep impression on me. When he handed me the money, he said, "You don't need to repay me, but be a good steward in how you use money and your opportunities. I will pray for you to be successful." Father Peter also gave me a note. "This is for Father Des Lauriers in Hong Kong. It is very likely he will have some work for you." The address and phone number were on the outside of the note.

Indeed, Father Des Lauriers gave me a part-time job and made it possible for me to attend the Catholic school. And on my birthday, he gave me *two* August moon cakes! Truly, these two Catholic Fathers provided for me what my own parents in their circumstances were unable to do through no fault of their own.

The father of friends of mine in Hong Kong prayed for me and counseled me to contact a Danish tramp steamer to find a job and passage to America. The captains of the *Laura Mærsk* became father figures for me. First, Captain Lindberg gave me clothing, shoes, and a separate room before promoting me to second waiter when he retired. Then Captain Obel came to the Customs Office in New York and defended me when I was accused of not having declared a gift I had brought for friends of Father Des. This support was unexpected and I was grateful. My respect for Captain Obel greatly increased.

In a way, the US Air Force provided for me for the four years that I served (from 1954 to 1958): I had plenty of delicious food; I had the finest clothes I had ever worn; I had comfortable accommodations, including a private room in the twenty-one months I was in the Philippines, and there were opportunities for taking college courses before I was discharged. And then I had the GI bill (both federal and California) which helped me go to college! Not only did God the Father provide for me through the various fatherly substitutes what my parents could not do, but He enabled me to financially help my mother and six younger siblings when they arrived almost penniless in Hong Kong in the fall of 1955.

My Relationship with My Mother

This is a painful section to write. My mother loved to play *mahjong* with her sister and friends, and she was very good at it. I loved to stay up late and watch this fascinating game until my mother would threaten to beat me if I did not go to bed. The stakes were small, but I suspect that the winnings helped my mother to keep us alive during the times when we had very little food. I do not remember any tenderness from her. She was superstitious; when I fell down the stairs on the first day of school, she kept me home for the rest of the year. She made me use my right hand to write or eat with chopsticks even though I was born left-handed.

The family photo on the previous page was taken before father left for America with Chuck (standing on a stool). Clock-wise around the parents are Yao-tim (Maria), George, Milly, baby Albert, Dolly, Philip, Robert and I.

I spent a lot of time hanging out with friends and amassed a gambling debt I tried to repay with odd jobs. In one instance when "scalping" movie tickets, I was threatened by thugs with beheading if I did not quit. All my siblings acknowledge our mother's quick temper and lack of patience, and the older ones remember the frequent hard end of the feather duster on our legs or behinds. When Pau-pau (grandmother) died, it hit me hard because she had at times stood between me and my mother's wrath.

After mother took Maria to Hong Kong and sent her on a ship chaperoned by priests to live with father (to cheer him up), she was left to raise the remaining seven children in Shanghai on very little money. Dad was only allowed by law to send a maximum of $100 per month. Mom had to be strong and completely self-reliant, and I feel she had become cold and hard as well. I regret that I did not step up as the oldest child still at home; instead of being a helper, my mother saw me as a burden and feared I would turn into a hooligan.

Escaping Shanghai

By 1952, hostile feelings against Americans were rising in China because of the Korean War—Americans were again portrayed as the bad guys. Posters in many stores accused the US of using biological weapons in Korea. Before he left for the US, Chuck used to regularly beat up an obnoxious Chinese boy in the neighborhood. Now the boy boldly took to cursing and calling us "bastard Americans." With feelings of impending doom, I was plotting day after day on how I could engineer my escape from Shanghai and make my way to America.

At the end of July, I had two essential documents in hand: the exit visa together with my birth certificate proving I was born in Kowloon, a city that was part of the British Crown Colony of Hong Kong. My mother told me that father had sent money to Hong Kong for my travel to the US. I purchased a one-way ticket to Lo Wu, the train station at the border of Communist China. Based on my birth certificate, I could enter and stay in Hong Kong indefinitely.

My mother and her sister accompanied me to the train station. As I was waiting in line to board the train, my aunt began to cry. She asked my mother, "Are you sad to see your son leave all by himself at such a young age?" My mother simply replied, "He has become unmanageable."

I did not say anything even though her indifferent demeanor cut my heart. Was she thinking, "I wish he had never been born"? She then turned to me and said, "Look up your cousin Ho Siu Hwa. She might put you up. She moved to Hong Kong about four years ago and is now married." This talk was entirely in Cantonese, as neither my mother nor aunt communicated in any other language or dialect.

When the train pulled out of the station, I felt a surge of immense anticipation and relief—I was ready for anything. I had some anxiety for sure, but no regrets. There was no ticket waiting for me in Hong Kong, even though for years my father insisted that he had sent the funds. This mystery was never cleared up. I was to earn my own way by working on a ship.

Later, when I had completed basic training in the Air Force as a radio operator, I was sent to the Philippines. At first, I was disappointed, but it turned out to be a blessing because I was frequently able to hitch-hike on flights to Hong Kong. Mom and my siblings had finally obtained exit visas from China after father had stopped sending support payments (at her request). As soon as I heard that they had arrived in Hong Kong, I was allowed to take a week of emergency leave. Mom cried when she saw me, saying that they had nowhere to live and were penniless. Mom and their bags had been thoroughly searched when they crossed the border, and an ornate carved table was confiscated. However, Mom was shrewd and had hidden some jewelry in the children's clothing—they were not searched.

I rented an apartment for Mom and my siblings and gave them all the money I had—enough for two months of food. The photo shows Robert, George, Milly, Albert, Mom, Dolly and Philip after they were settled in Hong Kong.

My cousin Ho Siu Hwa took me to the friends where my mother had found temporary shelter. She said to Mom, "You treated him as the worst child, and he has turned out to be the best child." There was no reply from Mom. But to this day cousin has kept up a special relationship with me. It is not easy to communicate with her, since now in her nineties she is hard of hearing, almost blind, and my Cantonese language skills have deteriorated.

As soon as I returned to Clark Air Force Base, I applied for an allotment from the US Air Force for my family, where I paid $65 per month, with the government matching this amount. This lasted until I mustered out of the Air Force to go to college. Then this support was continued under the GI bill during four years of college. After this, I continued to send regular monthly payments to my family for many years.

Neither my mother nor I ever apologized to one another for our mutual lack of emotional support. However, in later years, when I would visit, she slaved in a hot kitchen for a day to make me a stack of my favorite barbecued pork buns. I have never found anyone else to make them as tasty as she did.

I spent countless hours at the American Consulate wearing my uniform every time I was in Hong Kong, trying to help the process along, for my family to get visas to join father in the US.

After I was transferred stateside and was honorably discharged from active service in the Air Force, Father Des stayed in contact with the Consulate until the family left Hong Kong in 1960. Getting the visas for Mom (a Chinese citizen) and my siblings was extremely difficult—all except George were stateless since the law had been changed in 1941.

My sister Maria recently sent me this snapshot of our mother Ho Miao Ying and her surviving niece Ho Siu Hwa, dated 1934. I was surprised to see the family resemblance.

This brief summary of my early life differs from the published story of my childhood. It is because I finally have been able to share more of the pain, even though I'm still finding it difficult to think back to those times. I'm not close to my surviving siblings who all live in California and get together several times each year for family celebrations. Hunger pains have left a lasting memory, and I have a hard time when I have to wait for a meal. Understandably, I keep snacks close at hand.

On 15 August 1958, I was processed out of Travis Air Force Base in California, received my mustering-out pay and became a civilian again. I hitched a ride with an airman who was driving to San Francisco. My worldly possessions consisted of roughly $300 in my pocket and a duffle bag filled largely with military clothing and a few books. I closed my eyes as we left the base to avoid conversation.

Mentally, I reviewed the four years I had spent in the US Air Force. Although I did not achieve my dream of becoming a pilot, I learned to get along with people from all walks of life; I was trained to do a competent job; I found I could do well in college-level courses, and most importantly, I was able to provide for my family. I credited these achievements to my own efforts and good fortune—God was not in my life's frame of reference at this time.

Without a job, without a place to stay, without anyone who really cared about me, but with a head full of dreams and a heart full of hope, I brushed aside any doubts and feelings of apprehension. It was a new start, and I experienced emotions similar to the way I felt when leaving Shanghai six years earlier. I resolutely set my mind on looking forward. For me, America now was a land with open opportunities to get more education as a path to position, recognition, wealth and freedom. I would shortly be 21, an adult by any account. I was ready to step into the unknown and continue my quest of becoming a true American—it no longer seemed to be far out of reach.

Pastor Vernon Holstad, who reviewed a 2006 draft of my story, made the following comment, which still resonates: "Although circumstances and a combination of fear and love of adventure drove you, the real driving force in your life was unmet emotional needs that you experienced from birth, such as needs for love, nurture, affection, approval, affirmation, and security. Such needs are common to all people (especially high achievers)." I have to say that these needs, though often even hidden from my conscious self, influenced the choices that I made throughout my life.

Before I continue with my story, another thread from the past needs to be told. On a world map, the distance from Shanghai to California is a bit more than 6000 miles. Roughly 6000 miles in the opposite direction are Europe and Switzerland in particular. I find it fascinating that a wedding took place there in 1932, the same year that my parents met. A sailboat on Lake Zürich played an important part in that romantic story. My life would have been unimaginably different without the event that took place on that boat.

CHAPTER TWO

Monika: The Sailboat on Lake Zürich

Instead of telling the story of how my father, Angelo Amsler, met my mother, Rose Dällenbach, based on my memories, I want to use his own words, as written to his granddaughter, Anne, in a letter on April 1, 1986:

Until I was 23 years old, my five sisters fully satisfied my need for female companionship. Up to that time I had no close friendship with any girls and never kissed one before. Since I left the orphanage at age 21, I lived with my father in Zürich as the only one of his eight children. I had already started the fourth year of my work as a designer for water turbines in the world-renowned machine works Escher Wyss. My older brother (by 10 years) and I owned a sailboat, the St. Odille. *It was anchored at buoy at the lower end of Lake Zürich, about 60 meters from shore.*

Now it was Thursday, the 6th of August 1928, a beautiful hot summer day, which drew me after close of the office with all its might to the lake. Since my brother was away on vacation, I had free use of the boat. When I arrived with the dinghy at our anchored sailboat, I discovered to my great surprise on the far side of the boat's deck a sleeping girl wearing a swim belt made of cork pieces. Frightened awake by my handling of the boat, she stuttered a few words of apology for having climbed on the boat. She had swum across the lake and had gotten very tired because it was farther that she had expected. "Just stay, I will take you in a few minutes close to the other shore so you won't get tired again. Also, it's now dangerous here for swimming because the number of boats is increasing fast."

In a few minutes the sail was hoisted and the wind filled it and pushed the boat forward. Then she asked me what time it was. When I said, "a quarter past six," she became alarmed. By now I realized that the mermaid was nearer a young woman than a girl. She was supposed to be back at work by six; she was working as a cook in a mansion on

Mount Zürich. Because she spoke High German so well, I asked her if she was German. "No, I grew up in the Wallis, and my mother tongue is French. But I speak High German well because the people where I'm employed are German and also their children speak High German with me." This petite, good-looking young woman started to interest me, because she spoke two languages and could cook well. The 700 meters or so to the bathing station were traversed quickly, and so I asked her straightaway if I could invite her for a boat ride on the coming Saturday, but this time with clothes on. Two days after that I would have to go for 11 weeks of military service in the Ticino (in the southern part of Switzerland) to be promoted to corporal, so we wouldn't be able to meet for a long time. I must have impressed her, because she accepted my invitation for 8 p.m. on August 8.

To this first rendezvous in my whole life, I brought a lantern, because at night each moving boat had to have a light at the bow. Naturally we were not short of things to talk about, sharing each other's family and background. The wind died down. I asked this young woman—who would be twenty-one years old in a few days—if she had a beau. "No, I've never had one." This gave me the freedom to formally say, "I would be happy if you would grant me a kiss."

We sat on the steering bench. With the right hand I was holding the rudder, and with the left I was holding the rope from the big sail. After some hesitation this young woman stood up, bent down over me and put a very shy little peck on my left cheek. "Oh, not such a one like little children give each other in a game, I mean a real kiss on the mouth." Well, I did get one on the mouth, but did not find it exciting. I had to ask myself, why do people make all this fuss about kissing? While I was still thinking about this, a full moon was rising behind the hill across the lake.

In moments the water surface became very bright, and I did not see any other boats nearby. There still was no wind. So, I tied down the rope to hold the big sail steady. With my free hand, I reached for the hand of this young woman, pulled her gently to me, and now I kissed her on the mouth. I don't know how long we kissed each other then. However, I suddenly got shocked out of something heavenly by a strong shudder of the boat when it drove bow-first into the harbor wall at Enge. Neither of us had realized that the wind had come up. "Oh, thanks be to God that this obstacle was not another boat," I murmured and gave one more kiss. Then the boat traversed the 400 meters to the buoy in a moderate breeze. I accompanied Rose to her house by tram, and I walked another 20 minutes to my home.

Five days before the end of my military service, I came down with a high fever and was taken by ambulance to the hospital in Lugano. My friend Ernst Bossard had to pack up all my military gear which accompanied me to the hospital, and he shipped my dirty laundry to my father with a note of what had happened to me—to let him know why I was not coming home on October 20 as scheduled.

I had written "my dear girl" three days before I got sick that I would call her on the twenty-fifth to make a date for the following day. But by then, I was still in bed with a high fever and could not call her, nor write. When the twenty-sixth passed without hearing from me—it was her free Sunday afternoon—she became worried. She walked to my father's house to find out what had happened to her "cher Angelo." Fortunately, my father was home when this petite woman rang our doorbell and asked for me. When he showed her the note from my friend, she became even more anxious. Father wrote to me that same evening that "a small Fräulein asked after you today. Write to her soon." At that time, Father didn't have any idea I had this committed relationship that had only existed for eleven weeks but became deeper because of our correspondence.

On October 31, I was able to travel home, and on the following Sunday, finally our second date happened. My mother had died of a heart attack when I was only eight. My father, a traveling insurance salesman, could not cope with raising eight children, and neither could our grandmother. Therefore, the four youngest were placed in the city orphanage Entlisberg, where a pastor and his wife were in charge of fifty children. I lived there from 1914 to 1925. About a year later, my father moved into a tiny apartment by himself, and I rented a room (with board) from my second-oldest sister, Elly, who was married. This house had a large garden with a chicken coop. Thus, like when I was at the orphanage, I was able to do garden work again. This was a happy time, to which "my dear girl" made a big contribution.

During their years of courtship, the couple had to overcome the effect of Rose's back injury from a fall down a flight of stairs in the house where she was serving. She spent many months in a sanatorium. Elly strenuously objected to her—Rose was not good enough for her educated brother.

Shown here are Monika's Swiss maternal grandparents: Gottlieb Dällenbach (from Otterbach, Canton Bern) and Josephine Addy (from Martigny, Canton Valais). This is the only photo her mother had of her father who died in the pandemic of 1918 in Martigny, He was a school teacher. Her mother had to get a hard job in a mattress factory. When she remarried, the stepfather was unwilling to support five stepchildren. Rose had to drop out of school and go to work

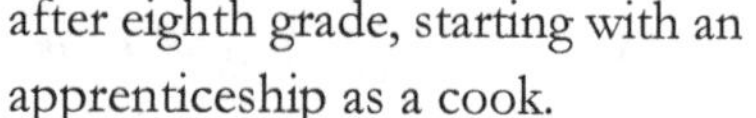

after eighth grade, starting with an apprenticeship as a cook.

Since Rose grew up in the French-speaking south-western part of Switzerland, she was a bit self-conscious about her German writing and speaking skills—never mind her lovely accent and cheerful, happy attitude as compared to the generally more morose Swiss-German people.

Angelo and Rose married in June 1932. By that time, he had already worked two years in Kriens for Bell Machine Works. Due to the deepening economic depression, jobs became scarce and salaries were cut again and again. For a few months, he worked in Thun in a small airplane design and construction firm. But when Bell recovered with new investors, he was rehired and stayed there until his retirement.

To the great joy of my parents, I was born in February 1939 and named Monika Marlies Edith. I had been a difficult forceps delivery and weighed only 2400 grams (5.3 lbs). My mother and I were in the Clinic St. Anna for two weeks. Here is a prescription for my care dated 10 March 1939: *Feeding: Mother's milk with supplement (thin rice gruel in a bottle). Six Meals: 5 and 9 am; noon; 4, 7 and 10 pm. Amount of Liquid: 80 grams (total per day = 470 grams).*

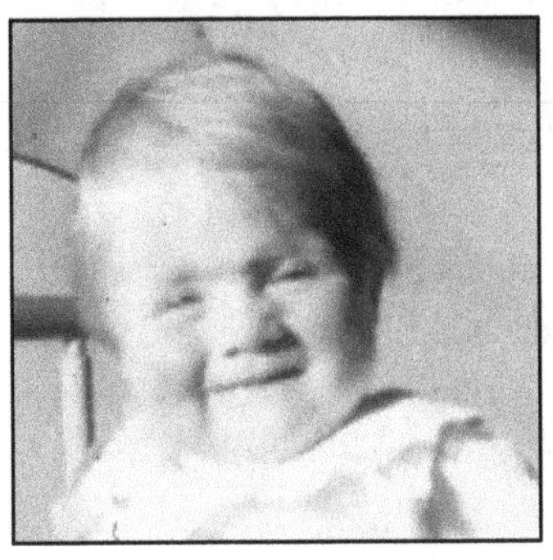

Christmas 1939 (shown in the next photo) was especially memorable for my parents. They had gone through a difficult time, with my father almost dying from a perforated appendix, and my mother suffering a miscarriage. This would have been a boy named Kurt. My mother was about six months pregnant now (with me sitting on her lap at ten months old), so my parents were counting their blessings, despite the growing fear of war. My sister Lili arrived three weeks before my first birthday. This was an early induced birth to save the life of our mother. Both Lili and I had blonde hair as toddlers, a common trait among many children in Europe.

My sister and I grew up with the love story of our parents in front of our eyes. In oils on a large canvas, my father had painted in blue shades the sailboat on the lake, with the rising full moon behind it. It hung in our living room. I see the lovely picture in its golden frame now above my sister's piano in our apartment, a sweet token of a romantic love that endured. Our father was faithfully devoted to his "dear girl" Rose all his life.

When she died of colon cancer at age 70, he was devastated. He was to live twenty more years but never even glanced at another woman. I was with him in the hospital, after he had surgery for a hernia. I read psalms and prayed for him. Then suddenly he became more alert; it reminded me of a soldiar at attention. He looked around, appearing to see astonishing visions of what I'm certain was heaven. Then he slowly stopped breathing. In a dream that night, I saw his siblings greeting him by saying, "What took you so long?"

Christmas was a special time for me while growing up. Real beeswax candles burned on the tree that had widely spaced branches. The tree would be decorated and lit on Christmas Eve. My sister and I believed that the Christ Child and his angels brought the tree. Our mother would take us for a walk, so our father could set it up in secret. After we returned home in the dark and heard a tiny bell tinkle in the living room, we could enter to marvel at the glorious lights. with the modest gifts under the tree. If we went to a Christmas Eve service at church, there would be a Christmas story (not necessarily the one from the Bible), and then all the children would get a "grittibänz" (a bread man with raisin eyes). I found this photo on the Internet, submitted by German "Chefkoch" Baldamus; it closely resembles the bread I remember, after I isolated and elongated it. Many that are sold in bakeshops are much fancier. Recipes are also available on the Internet.

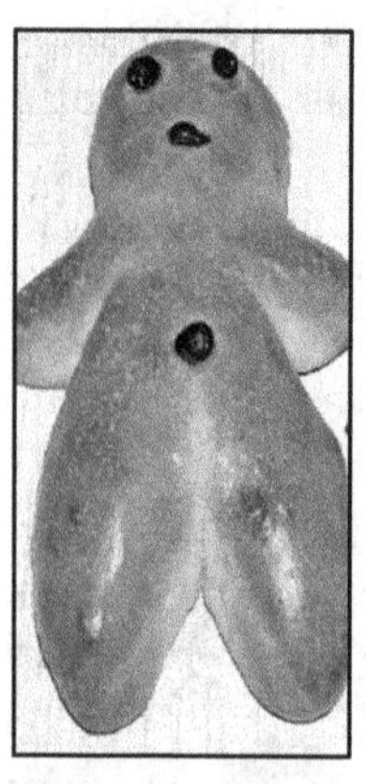

Thus Christmas for me was a very different experience from Edward's, where the only thing that made the day different was a special meal cooked by his mother, in respect for his father's Christian faith. Edward told me that his mother and grandmother together maintained a small Buddhist altar in their home.

CHAPTER THREE

Monika: A Girl Grows up in Switzerland

How do I wrap almost twenty years of my life into a few pages of description, and how do I select the best photos to illustrate the setting that influenced me? I want to give a glimpse of who I was as a child and provide enough detail to show the contrast with Edward's environment of growing up often very hungry in crowded war-torn Shanghai, a vast difference in culture that affected us later in our lives.

War Years

The first comparison would be the years of the Second World War. It broke out in Europe at the end of August 1939, when I was barely six months old. Within three days, more than 400,000 trained men were mobilized in Switzerland (about 20 percent of all employed persons). Switzerland remained neutral throughout the war, yet the war drastically changed life for everyone in this small country of four million people. By the spring of 1940, Switzerland was totally surrounded by nations at war: Germany with annexed Austria, conquered France, and allied Italy.

The soldiers were continuously upgraded and trained, not just for defending the border, but for defending the alpine redoubt (a final stronghold to preserve the country's independence). By 1943, Switzerland was considered to have the best prepared and equipped army for defense purposes. This went hand-in-hand with paying active soldiers 80% of the income they would have earned in the jobs they had to leave. The K31 rifle was standard issue from 1922 to 1958 and continued in partial use until 1970. Even today, it can be found in marksmanship competitions since the Swiss Karabiner Model 31 straight-pull bolt-action carbine rifle weighing 4 kg was known for its excellent accuracy and quality.

Why did Hitler not carry out his plan to overrun Switzerland and "squash the *Stachelschwein*" like he threatened to do? Swiss radio (like the BBC in England) was a perpetual annoyance to the Axis for broadcasting true reports about the progress of the war instead of German propaganda. Four factors are acknowledged as the main reasons:

1. The remarkable unity among the very diverse population showed a strong will to remain free and loyal to the homeland, at any price. The country had a long history of being neutral.
2. Since Switzerland had universal conscription with basic training at the age of 18 required of all able-bodied men and with yearly refresher courses to retirement age, it had a well-prepared army. The K31 rifles (including ammunition) and green uniforms were kept by all soldiers at home.
3. The alpine railway through the Gotthard—a direct link between Germany and Italy—was crucial to the war effort of the Axis. All strategic bridges and tunnels in Switzerland were mined. Valleys leading to mountain passes had concrete tank barriers with strategic bunkers and artillery emplacements in many mountainsides. In case of attack, this crucial rail line would have been destroyed. Instead, in trade for supplying Switzerland with coal, Germany could transport sealed rail boxcars (without inspection) on this alpine rail line from the German to the Italian border. At its peak, trains rolled in both directions every five minutes.
4. Switzerland was increasingly seen as more useful being neutral than being conquered with the threat of guerilla warfare, since its banks provided an essential service with gold and currency exchange. Swiss diplomats helped with peace negotiations among combatant countries, including the US and Japan. Conquest did not make economic sense.

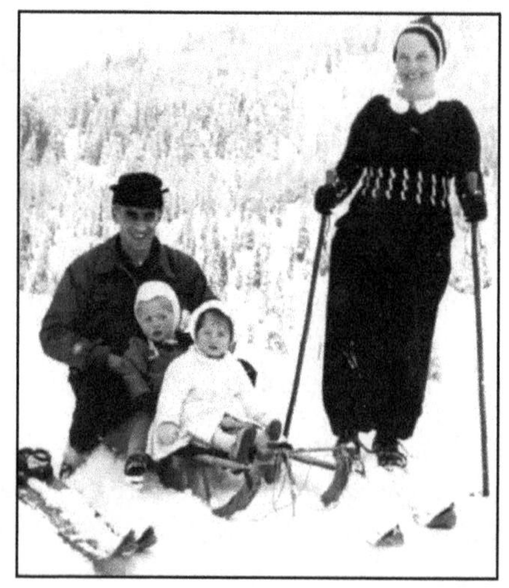

During World War II my father was away often as a corporal in the Swiss artillery in Biasca, guarding the southern Swiss border from Axis invasion. In the photo from Easter 1943 in Arosa during a brief leave, our parents look happy at the family's reunion, but my sister and I appear rather apprehensive about being in a strange place with our father whom we barely knew. His military records show that 1943 was the year he was away from home 124 days, and 105 days during 1944, for a total of 441 days by war's end.

Agriculture changed from cattle and milk production to grains, vegetables, and fruit. All arable areas were used, thus doubling the output. People's nutrition changed from meat to vegetables, potatoes and black bread, eventually extending to meatless weeks. Food was carefully allocated through rationing based on the requirements of various jobs; thus, public health was not seriously impaired, and nobody went hungry. Rationing eventually included sugar, oil, bread, pasta, milk, cheese, eggs, meat, shoes, and textiles. It decreased after the end of the war but did not stop entirely until 1948.

In the long, hard winter of 1941/42, energy for heating became a serious problem. Switzerland produced only a small amount of coal, peat, and wood. Allocations were small, and people had to get used to being cold. With Switzerland recognized as neutral, impartial, and honest, trade agreements were negotiated with many other countries. These agreements enabled imports of raw materials, fuels, and food, together with export of machinery, pharmaceuticals, and chemicals, thus maintaining the Swiss economy with only moderate inflation. My daily job was to fill a bucket with coal in the cellar and carry it to our stove in the kitchen, whenever it was empty and I was strong enough.

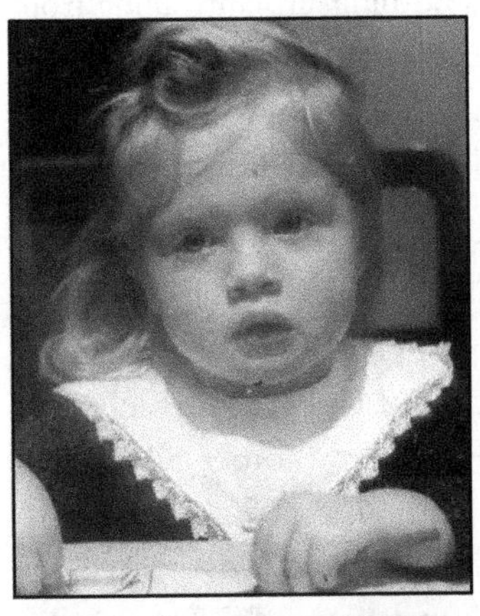

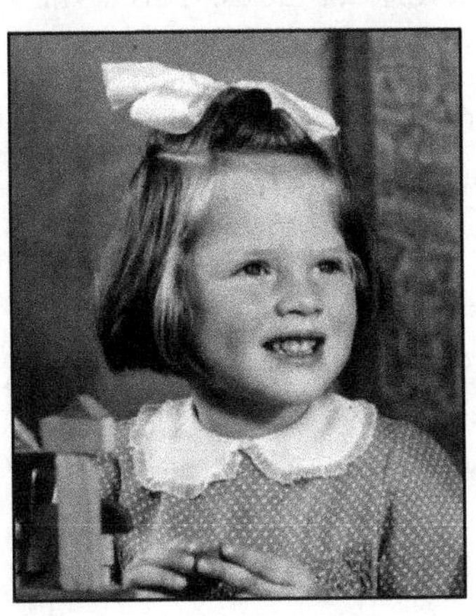

The two photos show me with my favorite activities: drawing and building with blocks. I still have that box of small wooden blocks. My mother laughingly told her friends that I disliked chocolate as a child. When someone gave me a first bite around age 2, I spit it out immediately.

Despite the war, my parents did their best to keep our home life routine and peaceful. They rented a garden plot to grow extra vegetables, especially potatoes, onions, and string beans. My mother dried the string beans. In the winter, when soaked and then cooked with a small piece of bacon and potatoes, they became one of my favorite meals. The onions were braided together and hung to dry in our cellar.

Once a month, my mother walked with my sister and me to the county courthouse to pick up the ration cards. Sometimes she traded our bread coupons for milk coupons with the family living upstairs—they had five hungry boys. One day, my father brought home a crate full of canned sardines provided by his company, a cause for a celebration. With meat being scarce, these oily sardines provided many nutritious meals when served with brown bread or potatoes.

During these war years we did have blackouts, and nightly we saw the searchlights in the sky from a military airfield in nearby Emmen. Once, while out on a Sunday afternoon walk, we observed a burning airplane falling from the sky. My father took me on a tour of an American bomber at Emmen. The friendly officers wore khaki uniforms. Any aircraft violating Swiss air space was brought down and its crew interned for the duration of the war.

I had terrifying nightmares around the time I was five or six. I did not talk about them with my parents, and I have no idea where these images came from. I dreamed of being captured by soldiers in grey, being spray-painted with a blue stain, being stuffed into an open metal garbage can, and then being tossed into a large truck with others. Did I hear my mother talking with her neighbors about the Jews being rounded up in Germany and taken to concentration camps? Or did I learn about this from radio broadcasts my parents listened to at noon and at six o'clock during our meals? This is still a puzzle for me.

All the church bells rang when the war in Europe ended, and Mami took us on a day's celebratory excursion on a steamer on Lake Lucerne sponsored by my father's company while he was in bed with the flu.

We lived in the middle apartment in a three-story building. These houses, some in chalet style, were surrounded by gardens and fruit trees. Both my parents loved gardening for growing vegetables, berries, and flowers. One of the best rewards was for us to eat tomatoes right from the vine, as shown in the following photo. Instead of helping my mother on Fridays with cleaning our apartment, I could choose to do weeding in the garden!

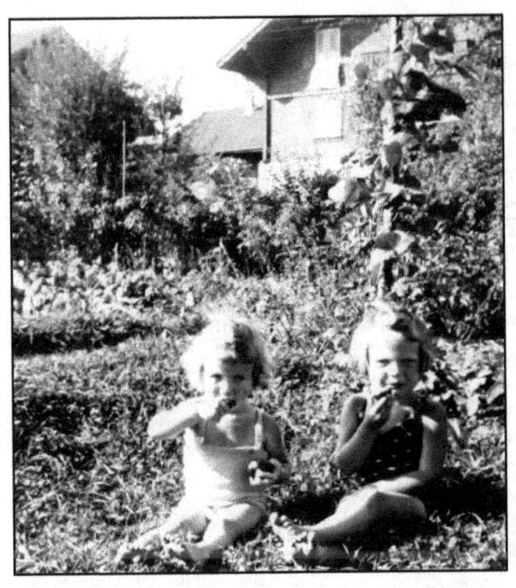

During the summer, my mother would place two large laundry tubs on the small lawn and fill them with water. When the sun had warmed the water, we could take a bath—a special treat on a hot afternoon. We always had views across green meadows and forested hills into high mountain peaks, something I would come to miss years later, when I lived in the Detroit area. Apart from those nighmares, our well-ordered life gave us a sense of security, especially after my father was able to return to his steady job. This is in stark contrast to the chaotic and dangerous life Edward had to endure in Shanghai.

Elementary School

My experiences with school were also different from those Edward had in China. The year I started school, I caught many childhood diseases—perhaps because my mother had been very protective of us and rarely permitted us to play with kids in the neighborhood before we went to school. We did not attend the optional kindergarten. Thus, we were not exposed to many illnesses except sore throats. The frequent throat infections were the reason I had to have my tonsils out when I was six, and I was in the hospital for five days. During first grade, which started after Easter when I was seven, I was home for over 100 days with chicken pox, a very bad case of whooping cough, the flu, and measles.

While in sixth grade, I caught pneumonia. I thought I was going to die and was too weak to care. The doctor came to our house every day, and some special, bitter antibiotic pills were ordered from America to save my life. The home remedy tried first for a chest cold was usually a hot poultice made from fried onions. An even stronger natural treatment Edward and I had in common was a mustard plaster (a thick poultice made with flour and ground up mustard seeds especially for bronchitis).

My sister and I had a fifteen-minute walk from home to the schoolhouse for the first two grades, with an extra five minutes uphill to a five-story building for the upper grades. Our father also came home for lunch (the main meal of the day), and he had a 20-minute walk. He had a 44-hour work week, with a half-day on Saturday. We kids had Wednesday and Saturday afternoons off. We had quite a bit of homework with little time to play, except during vacations.

My sister and I loved it when our father carved us little sailboats from pine bark while on a hike. He cut the sails from postcards, and we floated the boats down a creek. Sometimes he helped us build a dam to keep the boats from being swept away too quickly.

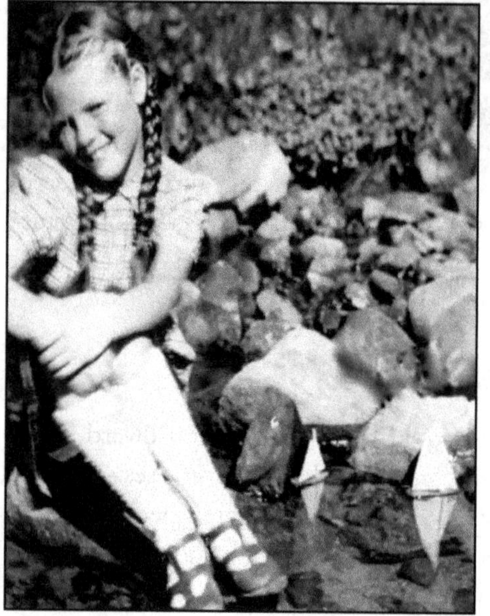

The first four grades were co-ed. I got disciplined a few times by a whack or two across my knuckles with a 1 cm-square wooden ruler for talking in class. There was a dark isolation cell for disobedient kids, and the fear of it ensured that I tried to be well behaved.

We had slates in wood frames to practice writing. While I was sick, the class had learned cursive writing. When I was back in school after two months, the elderly teacher just told me to copy the writing that I saw on the blackboard—he did not give me any special instruction. I blame my terrible handwriting for this—I never got more than an acceptable grade of 5 (out of a maximum of 6) for handwriting, not even in high school. I did not like the third/fourth grade teacher much, even though his wife and my mother were friends. During those years my name by my schoolmates and family was abbreviated to Moni. Then the boys changed the intonation *to mooh-nee*, which was the Swiss-German word "*Muni*" for bull or ox. I hated it! I remember that classroom as being dark and dreary—even in the weekly drawing class, we could only use pencils or charcoal but no colors.

Below is a photo of my fifth/sixth-grade classroom in Kriens, a bright space on the fifth floor facing the playground and the Catholic Church with a large clock on its bell-tower. My friend Louise Bodmer is seated directly in front of our teacher Miss Nina Schmid (in dark dress), and I'm standing on Louise's left. We girls all wore aprons to protect our dresses. This was a necessity in those days before housewives had washing machines. Each student still had a slate and chalk for writing; it was often used for arithmetic problems. We had nibs and inkwells for writing on paper, although most writing was with pencil. It took me a year to persuade my father that I *really* needed to have a fountain pen for writing. Then Lili got one the first time she mentioned it, which I found eminently unfair.

Drawing class improved in fifth grade in that we could use color pencils. Miss Schmid would put a simple colored line-drawing on the blackboard and indicate all dimensions. We had to copy it exactly. There was no freedom to be creative! What a difference it is for my grandchildren with the special art classes, materials, and techniques now available. I can't imagine that finger painting, water colors, or markers would have been allowed—too messy!

One class was in a special room with skylights at the top of the building. This was for the sewing class which all girls had to take one afternoon a week from third grade up. Much time was spent teaching us how to mend holes in knitted socks and rips in fabrics, so the repair would be almost invisible. Another skill I still use was making beautiful button holes and sewing on buttons. We didn't get to use sewing machines until the upper grades.

Of course, we also learned how to knit—I still remember how to do the heel of socks. I'm thankful my mother taught me how to knit intricate doilies, how to tat (*frivolité* in French), and how to crochet and do cross-stitch and other embroidery. Because people don't use doilies on their furniture anymore, I have converted many of mine into framed wall hangings. Now, these handicrafts have mostly disappeared, and my eyes are no longer sharp enough. This is one cultural change I regret with nostalgia. On the other hand, I have much joy in wildflower photography with a digital camera given to me by my children on my eightieth birthday! With the photos downloaded and viewed on a large computer screen, impaired eyesight is not a handicap, and I can edit the photos in PowerPoint.

In sixth grade, we could check out one library book every two weeks. When Louise and I traded books because we were fast readers, we were punished by not being allowed any other books for the rest of the year! Louise and I had volunteered to take care of the flowers in our classroom but got into trouble when we poured water on boys below the window during recess. We were called to the principal's office and sternly reprimanded. We lost the flower job, but when no one else volunteered, Miss Schmid gave us back the job for the rest of the school year. What I most appreciate about her, even after all these years, is that she stopped the class and led us in a prayer during thunderstorms. I kept in touch with her after she retired, and I learned that she regularly prayed for her former students.

Secondary School and High School

This passport photo was taken ahead of our family going on a vacation to Italy in 1952. Shortly after this, my mother allowed me to have my hair cut short. By this time, I had started the first year of secondary school. I had done well on the entrance exam. Less gifted students were required to continue to the regular seventh and eighth grade, before they could move on to an apprenticeship. However, there was an opportunity to take the entrance exam again after seventh grade, and if the scores were good, the student could switch to the secondary school track. This is what my sister Lili did. From then on, she was an excellent student.

The first two years of secondary school had separate classes for boys and girls. I don't remember much about them, except that a beloved teacher died of cancer at mid-year. The optional third year was co-ed since there were only twelve girls, and we had to sit in the back rows. I did well in all academic subjects. My favorite was drawing, and we had an excellent teacher for the once-a-week art class. Based on an elaborate drawing I made of a medieval town, he said I had architectural talent. I really learned about perspective, composition, and drawing accurate details—very useful when years later I designed solar houses.

After I had learned to read at age 7, I was allowed to read my parents' newspapers and magazines which I did avidly. During the second year of high school, I discovered the *Biggles* youth-oriented adventure series about a pilot, written by W.E. Johns. I did not have a clue about what I wanted to do with my life, although I dreamed about being a pilot. Since there was no hope of employment for women as airline pilots in those days, I thought that crop dusting in Peru might be a possibility. I never even considered that I might get married and have a family. Now I'm glad God had other plans for me.

I have many memories of excursions and vacations in the mountains. Lili would accompany our father on strenuous hikes, while I would sit with my mother in the hotel's garden and read. She suffered from altitude sickness and did not feel well in the high mountains. As for me, it took a couple of weeks each summer to build up my energy due to the anemia which plagued me during childhood, despite the vitamin tablets, cod liver oil, and sunlamp treatments I received during the winters.

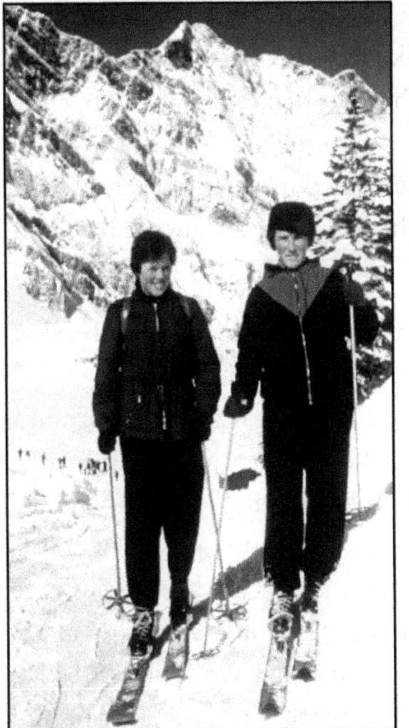

Lili was an elegant skier, whereas I was awkward and slow. After a day on the slopes, I would be utterly exhausted. I was barely able to keep up with my classmates during the hiking week with our school each summer, starting with fifth grade, and then during three ski camps when I was in high school.

A special Sunday excursion was spring-skiing from Jochpass to Trübsee above Engelberg. We had to get up around four to go by tram from Kriens to Lucerne, where we boarded a small motorboat to Stansstad. From there, a narrow-gage train took us to Engelberg. After a ten-minute walk, we rode a funicular up a steep hill, followed by an aerial cable car to Trübsee. Then we could ski down to cross the frozen lake (seen in the photo on the previous page) to reach the long ski lift up to Jochpass. If it was cold, our father made us drink hot chocolate or tea in the warming hut, before we could get on the slopes. We also ate our picnic lunch on the hut's sunny terrace. In early afternoon came the long descent by ski all the way back to Engelberg.

Both my strict parents and the village culture led me to be cautious and take few risks. Neighbors were always on the lookout and would report any unseemly behavior to my parents, so this encouraged behaving "by the rules." Adults were also scrutinized by their neighbors; housewives wouldn't dare omit airing the feather quilts on the sills of open windows every morning in good weather, or they would be talked about as being lazy or incompetent. I remember when getting home from school, my mother would have already been informed if I had neglected to greet one of the neighbors, having walked along day-dreaming. I refused to try beer or smoke cigarettes when tempted by peers in high school.

I did learn how to ride a rusty men's bike that belonged to the boy who lived in the apartment below us. The bike had no brakes, resulting in a spill and skinned knees when I could not leap off wearing a full skirt. My taking this risk had a good outcome: my father persuaded my favorite aunt to give me her bicycle. I used it throughout my high school years and later for going to work.

I still find it incredible—and so very admirable—that by the time Edward was sixteen, he had survived in a large city during chaotic wartime; he had already been on his own, helped support his family from his meager earnings, and had some strong goals (and dreams) for his life. It was not until years later that I came to appreciate the strict and protected life I had in my family. For example, when I took a first-aid training course at the police station in Lucerne when I was eighteen, my father accompanied me there and picked me up afterwards. During my teen years, I was sometimes so upset at my parents' restrictions that I seriously considered running away. I planned what items I would take along in my backpack. But when I realized I could not bring any of my books, I abandoned the idea of leaving. Edward's life in this one respect was easier—he had few possessions.

Nature was close to home for me. My mother had flower boxes with geraniums on the ledge of a balcony. Each year, a pair of blackbirds (*Amsel* in German) would build a nest in one of the boxes. When a cat caught one of the birds in the garden and injured its wing, my sister and I packed it up carefully in a softly lined shoebox with air holes punched on two sides. Then we took it to the post office and mailed it to the bird observatory (Swiss Ornithological Institute) at Sempach for treatment, where it arrived the same afternoon.

This incident is a sweet memory of when Lili and I were cooperating. We were very different in temperament; she was more emotional and much stronger than I. Often I would end up at the short end of a physical disagreement. Also, I learned from our mother—known as a peacemaker—to keep quiet and not get involved in arguments that I could not win. I could not believe it when Lili learned to swim one afternoon in the summer of 1946 when she was six. About an hour later, I finally accomplished the same feat—although I was a year older.

During the time Edward was in technical training in the US Air Force, I completed the third year of secondary school. Most students at this stage in Switzerland would then choose a career track and enter an apprenticeship with trade school in their chosen field. Alternately, a year for language training could be undertaken first, either in a boarding school or as an au-pair working with a family. The preferred locations were either the French-speaking part of Switzerland or England. Very few girls were supported for advanced education—most families considered it a wasted expense since typically girls would marry and raise a family instead of having a career. Mainly, only two professional careers were open for girls at that time: elementary school teaching or nursing, neither of which attracted me. In China, the culture was similar in this regard. Edward's parents were unusual in that they encouraged their daughters to be well-educated.

I wanted to learn more but had no inclination towards a particular field of study. Because I passed the entrance requirements, my parents enrolled me in the Commercial High School for Girls (STH) in Lucerne. This was a three-year program resulting in a diploma. From there the path would be open for a good secretarial position or possibly entrance to a technical school (although none of us thought ahead that far). To avoid paying the out-of-town tuition rate, my parents decided to move from Kriens to an older, rather gloomy apartment in Lucerne for the next three years. This move gave me access to the city library in Lucerne. The adult son of the family that lived in the upstairs apartment was a Swissair pilot, and he lent me his books about flying.

Overall, I enjoyed high school and graduated at the top of the class. French had been the greatest challenge, and I had to study hard to get top grades by the end of the three years. Incredibly, to this day I have occasional nightmares about not being prepared for a tough French exam.

What I appreciated most about high school was the coordinated curriculum. When we studied a certain time period in history, we would simultaneously examine its literature, architecture, and art. This is also the first time I had to present a book report. As the subject, I chose the impressionist painter Paul Gauguin. In my entire college career, I never encountered such a coordinated learning environment—what a pity! Of course, living in Europe, paintings, architecture, and the settings for different periods in literature in their respective countries and languages are close at hand for memorable illustrations. More cultural enrichment came with the season tickets my parents had for the playhouse in Lucerne. I was able to see a number of operas such as *Rigoletto, Carmen,* and *The Magic Flute*, as well as tragedies such as *King Lear.*

My parents did not think much of going to the movies. I only remember my mother seeing *Gone with the Wind* with friends. As a family, we saw Walt Disney's *The Living Desert.* I begged my father to take me to *Reach for the Sky,* a true story of a Royal Air Force pilot who had lost both legs in an airplane accident and went on to fly countless missions during WWII. As a German POW he made many escape attempts. I saw it twice!

Of the fifteen girls in my high school class, one came to be a life-long friend. Brigit König invited me to spend a week of summer vacation with her family in the Jura above Tramelan in a rented cottage. I was surprised my parents let me go, allowing me to travel there by train on my own. I hiked, played games, stretched out in a hammock, and lugged groceries in backpacks for an hour up the mountain with peals of laughter with Brigit and her younger brother, Walti.

This sweet photo shows me as a teenager with my mother and my Grandmaman who only spoke French.

After high school graduation just before Easter 1958, I accepted a position as a secretary and receptionist in the Official Tourist Office in Lucerne, with the stipulation that I would be allowed to break my contract if I received an invitation to study in America. My boss did not think this likely when my father inserted this stipulation, so he signed the amended contract. I believe my father knew me better than I knew myself and recognized that I was suffering from a case of "ache for far-away places"—the opposite of being homesick.

I was amazed that my father allowed me to take flying lessons in a Piper Cub at the small airfield in Kägiswil during that summer. I paid for the lessons with my earnings from my job. I had to buy a pair of capris (called pedal pushers in those days) from a classmate who lived in our neighborhood in Lucerne and with whom I had taken early morning hikes before school on the Sonnenberg. I passed the test flight and exam after thirty-six and a half hours of flight time.

The scariest moment had been when I got delayed on a solo cross-country flight and had to land in semi-darkness on the home field (without lights and radio)—not easy with tall trees and a river just before the runway and barbed wire on the sides recently installed by the rather unfriendly neighboring farmer. One day, when I hit this fence and tore a gash in the tail of the plane, two colleagues and I ended up patching the damage instead of flying.

Here is a photo of the cross-country flight I made right after getting my private pilot's license in August 1958. With a colleague from the office, I flew to Yverdon to visit my sister Lili and our Aunt Ida. The weather became stormy. I could stay the night with my sister in her dorm at the school where she was learning French. My colleague took a train back to Lucerne, so she would not miss work the next morning. I didn't show up until noon since I had to fly the plane back to Kägiswil. My boss couldn't say much; the bookkeeper at the travel office was also the accountant for my Aero Club.

Looking back, what lifelong skills did I learn while growing up? From my father I learned some carpentry. He had built our first refrigerator and did some hydraulic tests in our bathtub with a model of a penstock for a Kaplan turbine. Then he let me use the left-over boards to make myself a small bookshelf. He also taught me how to use a slide rule. I was so proud when I figured out how to fix the lamp and dynamo on my bike. All the arithmetic drills in school might have been boring, but I still add and subtract in my head or on paper (in German) faster than doing these sums on a calculator.

Here is another story about how protected I was in my teens. Our youth group at church had a weekend in the mountains with strict chaperones and separate lodging for boys and girls. During a hike across alpine meadows, Franz—a handsome fellow—picked a bouquet of *alpenrosen* for me. He was a year older than me and an auto-mechanic apprentice. Sometime later, in the process of developing a budding friendship, we went swimming in Lake Lucerne (with my sister Lili along). At this stage, I was not ready to be kissed.

Then my father wanted to meet Franz and had a very long talk with him. I learned years later that one of my father's sisters had gotten pregnant as a teenager while at the orphanage. She then had an abortion because the boyfriend's mother was mentally ill. Anyway, that was the end of my having a boyfriend—he was thoroughly scared off by my father. However, there is a sweet sequel. When Edward and I were in Switzerland with our children in 1971, our youngest son broke his collar bone, and I had to take him to a pediatrician. A pretty German mother was in the waiting room with a little boy who resembled Franz and had the same last name. I didn't speak to her, but I think God let me know that Franz had a nice family.

This photo shows the view of our church and Mt. Pilatus that I had from my bedroom window. My parents had moved back to Kriens after I graduated from high school. By then, it took me four hours to climb from home to the top of the mountain (and about half that time to get back).

How I came to be in Ventura, California two weeks after that flight to Yverdon is an amazing chain of events which I now see as God's providence. I recently found a dusty folder with old letters. Excerpts from them will tell most of the story, which mainly took place during my last year of high school and a few months of working in the tourist office.

CHAPTER FOUR

Monika: Trail to a Student Visa

Lucerne was the host city of the big Rotary International Convention in May 1957. My high school class was drafted to help with the typing, mimeographing, and registration. Fourteen girls could work at the registration desk, while one was relegated to a dark, crowded cubicle for filing. To be impartial, our teacher Mr. Fritz Wyss drew lots and pulled my name out of his hat for the filing job. My classmates laughed at this outcome—I had been the teacher's pet. In the photo, I'm the girl in black. As a reward for our work, we were invited to attend a session where Helen Keller was the main speaker.

In front of us sat a friendly American family—they were very interested in us and asked many questions about who we were and why we were there. Walking back to the filing job, I thought of inviting this family to my home. I only remembered their hometown of Ventura, but this was enough to find their name and their hotel in the files. On the way back to school, I stopped at their hotel. They were not in, but I left a note with my telephone number and best time to call. On my way home from school, it sank in what I had done on the spur of the moment, and I was apprehensive of what my parents would say when I confessed my deed. I had some hope that my invitation would be ignored by Arthur and Esther Langford. Actually, I was rather astonished that I had done this—as normally I was rather timid with strangers.

However, Art and Esther Langford, with their daughter Artie, were thrilled at this opportunity to visit a Swiss home—they were very interested in international relations. I had to pick them up at the hotel since I was not confident that they could find our address. What was a short walk uphill for me was found to be rather taxing by these Americans who were used to driving everywhere. We spent a nice evening together with my father showing slides of Switzerland and my mother serving cake and tea.

I met with the Langfords one more time before they left Switzerland, and we stayed in touch with our new American friends through letters. I loved having the photo they gave me during their visit.

Here is the letter Mr. Langford wrote to his Rotary Club in Ventura on May 9, 1957 on stationary from the Grand Hotel Flora in Rome, Italy:

Dear Doug and the Exchange Student Committee:

We arrived here in Rome OK after a wonderful trip down the Italian Riviera. Your letter and Club Bulletin were waiting for us. I notice that you, Doug, have set up a committee on an exchange student and I know that we have talked about doing this thing for some years. Esther and I have been discussing this same thing here on this side, for a perfect situation has fallen into my lap. Here are the details:

At the convention session on youth student exchange activities, a group of young girls from the Lucerne high school sat directly behind us and we made friends with them and helped them with the English interpretations which were mimeographed of all the speakers.

That evening, upon returning to our own hotel we found a note inviting us to the home of one of the girls to "see" how a regular Swiss family lived. Of course, we grasped the opportunity and the evening was most informing and interesting. This girl is an honor student in the commercial classes that did the typing and mimeographing for the whole Convention. She is very sharp and speaks three languages and will be a student in the last year of high school at 18 years of age.

I think she would make an excellent choice and we would know what we are getting. I find that she is anxious to come to the US and work after her graduation, but I know that it is very difficult to get a US visa for this purpose. She has already started her application, and I think she would jump at the chance to attend our high school and finish her senior year.

I strongly feel this is a wonderful opportunity for our club and we should do it now!
Sincerely, Art

I did not know of this effort by Mr. Langford. I wrote to him on June 5, using my fountain pen with green ink, that I had heard from the American Consulate General. It was impossible to give me an appointment for my formal application earlier than 13 to 15 months from that time, which would mean around August 1958. I also would have to furnish documentary proof of one of the following: all personal resources I had available in the US, or details of employment waiting for me with an adequate income, or an affidavit of support by friends or relatives residing permanently in the US. Then I continued:

I will be frank. I don't like to ask you for this affidavit, and I don't want to trouble you with this. I would like to see you again, but how shall I without the visa? I hope that you are not angry about my impertinent letter. I have decided not to go to a college but to work in an office if possible, to learn American business, or to work in a home for learning about an American household. … My parents thank you very much for your letter. They said that their new friends have much changed their opinion of the Americans, and this for the best.

On August 24, 1957 I followed this up with a handwritten letter in green ink, two weeks after I had started my practicum (internship) at the Official Tourist Office in Lucerne. I had learned from the Consulate that with an immigration visa I could work *and* study. But with a student visa I would only be allowed to study and would have to return to Switzerland—I could not apply for immigration status while in the US.

On October 6, I typed a letter to Mr. Langford, letting him know I had a job offer in Switzerland after high school graduation (to the end of September 1958). I wondered if I should write to the Ventura Rotary Club, "If I were to be selected for the club's scholarship, would I get a student visa?"

Here follows a letter hastily written in pencil on lined note paper by Mr. Langford, dated 14 October 1957:

Dear Monica:
Your second letter arrived a few days ago, and I'm sorry not to have answered the first. We have been very, very busy harvesting a bumper apple crop here on our ranch. We have picked about 20,000 bushel boxes of apples and made 17,000 gallons of apple juice. It will take about 4 more weeks to finish the harvest as we shall have about 30,000 bushels.

The weather has been very hot this September and October and we have had to work 10-12 hours per day 7 days per week, so you will realize that we had not much time to write letters.

As to the possibility of your coming to America, I definitely support that you do not come and try to work, as business is on the down trend and jobs will be harder and harder to get. I doubt if our Rotary club will want to provide enough money to bring you here to Ventura to school as I have been unable to sell the members on such a large cost. I am suggesting that you write to the following and your chances of a year's study in America would be better than with our local club: American Field Service and Institute of International Education (see addresses below). I understand these two organizations help foreign students to come to the US, and they can be of help to you. In the meantime, I shall continue to get the Ventura Club interested.
Most sincerely, Arthur P. Langford

On December 11, 1957 I wrote to Mr. Langford, letting him know that I would be working at the Official Tourist Office in Luzern the following summer. This would enable me to pay for my own airfare to America, thus eliminating a large expense for the sponsoring families or the Rotary Club.

On April 2, 1958 I wrote again in green ink. The original letter in the folder has a big water stain and is only partially legible:

Dear Mr. Langford,
Herewith I'm sending you a copy of my diploma of the Commercial High School for Girls, Lucerne, which I got two days ago. It was better than I had expected. I, with two other girls, tied for first rank, and I won two prizes. … Please note that we have a new

address, as my family moved to a sunny apartment in Kriens, right across from our church and with a beautiful view of Mt. Pilatus.

Yours faithfully, Monika Amsler

The next letter in the file is also handwritten—just a small note in green ink, dated May 23, 1958. It is addressed to Mr. Langford:

Three days ago, your friends, Mr. and Mrs. Smith, brought me your greetings. I was very much surprised to hear from you. They were very nice. It was a great pleasure for me to see somebody from your town.

Last Saturday I took my first lesson for flying. I think it's wonderful that my father has allowed me to take the lessons. My flying instructor is Mr. Häfliger, the most famous Swiss test pilot. It is a big thing to fly with him. I'm now able to fly turns and figure eights of my own.

Have you got the copy of my diploma? May I ask you to write me, if there is any possibility that I can come to America this fall or not? You see, I've now to tell Mr. Ed Schütz, the manager of my office, when I want to leave in the fall, early or late? What shall I tell him? I would be so glad if you would answer me immediately.

Yours sincerely, Monika Amsler

I want to mention that the remaining flying lessons, until I got my license, were with Mr. Huber, since Mr. Häfliger was in a serious airplane crash. Next comes a typed letter from me, dated July 16, 1958:

Dear Mr. Langford,

I have been very much surprised to have a letter from you. But when I read it, I saw that there was such a great joy for me that I do not know how to thank you for it. It is with very great pleasure that I am accepting your invitation. I wish I could thank you enough for all the work and all the pains you surely had to get it to me, and I will do every effort to justify your kind decision.

Now I'm looking forward to see you and Mrs. Langford and Artie again, and to learn about your life and the thinking of American people. All this is so thrilling for me, I can do nothing but think of it all day and hardly can I believe that it is true.

As soon as I'll get the information about Ventura College, I shall write you again and tell you, which courses I would like to attend, and the date of my arrival and all my further steps in this matter. Today, I wrote to the American Consulate about the student visa. I also told my boss, the manager of the Official Tourist Office, Dr. Ed Schütz, of my plans. He is a Rotarian, too, and very interested in them, and he said he will help me.

I am very glad and grateful to you, that you give me this opportunity to learn about the United States and to become acquainted with other people. Thank you once more a thousand times for your invitation and your help to me. I should like also to thank your Rotary Club for this generous proposal, I shall write them as soon as possible.

Give Mrs. Langford and Artie all my best wishes, I am very happy that I can see you and your family within a few weeks and that I may stay with you.

Sincerely yours, Monika Amsler

Next in the file I found a letter my father wrote to Mr. Langford on July 1, 1958. He used formal stationary with his printed letterhead.

Dear Mr. Langford,

I thank you very much for your letter of 8th inst. It is with great pleasure that I accept your invitation for my daughter to come to California. I am glad for her, that you succeeded in getting her this scholarship. It is for that reason I allow her to accept your proposal and to go to Ventura. I shall pay the round-trip air fare to your town, as well as some pocket-money so that she will be able to pay the daily expenses herself.

It is not easy for parents to know such a young daughter so far away from home. Your kindness to look after her as to a daughter of yours gives me great satisfaction. I am sure that she will be in good hands. I thank you for all the trouble you have had till today for my daughter, and I hope that she will be able to reward your further support with real friendship with your daughter. Please give my thanks also to Mrs. Langford and Artie, because they too will have to look after her, and will have troubles.

Hoping that this experience will be for both families a very pleasant one, I remain, dear Mr. Langford, with best wishes to Mrs. Langford and Artie,

Very sincerely yours, A. Amsler

Then I was surprised to find a formal letter in the file dated July 29, 1958. It was typed on thin official airmail stationary and was addressed to Mr. Arthur P. Langford, Chairman of International Student Activities. It was written by my boss, Dr. Ed Schütz.

I was very much in awe and perhaps even somewhat afraid of him. He was a perfectionist and not very forgiving when his employees made any mistakes; and he regretted handing out praise when it was followed shortly after by some shortcoming. What made me most uncomfortable above all in my job was answering the telephone.

Re: Miss Monica Amsler, one-year's education at Ventura College

Dear Mr. Langford,

Thank you for your kind letter of July 23, from which we note that Miss Amsler is supposed to arrive in Ventura around the twentieth of August. Miss Amsler being engaged in our seasonal staff by agreement until the end of September and the month of August being our top season, we actually see no way to dismiss her as early as that.

We are however willing to meet half-way and Miss Amsler will therefore be free of duty as of September 6. You may be assured that any assistance that may become necessary will be rendered to Monica. Financial help will not become necessary as her travelling expenses are paid by Mr. Amsler._We do not doubt that Miss Amsler will become a true member of the Rotary Family and we thank you in advance for whatever support you will kindly lend her during her visit in Ventura.

Only three letters remained in the file: a typed one from me dated July 31, 1958, then a letter from the Dean of Students at Ventura College dated August 6, 1958, and a final handwritten note from me dated August 15, 1958, written as usual in green ink. I am still amazed at how quickly the paperwork needed fell into place, just in the nick of time. At work, I was too busy with selling tickets for the International Music Festival to worry about anything else.

Dear Mr. Langford, dear Mrs. Langford, dear Artie,

It was with great pleasure that I got your letters and I am so happy that I can see you and that I can stay with you. I thank you very much again. But I am now so sorry that I have to tell you that I cannot leave here as soon as you have wished me to come, because Dr. Schütz won't let me go as early as this. I am very very much disappointed and I hope very much that you will accept me nevertheless and that you will not be too angry. I tried everything, but I couldn't change his decision. But he will give me a good introduction into Rotary.

If I shall be free at noon on September 6, I will try to book a flight to leave Zürich in late afternoon, to arrive in Los Angeles (with the SAS polar route) on Sunday, September 7, at 13:00 California time. But I am now worrying about my registration at Ventura College, because I think that I'll be too late. I have received your brochures on the College, and I was very surprised because it was much bigger than I thought it to be. It is difficult to choose the right subjects. …

In the meantime, I received a lot of forms from the American Consulate. May I ask you to help me get two things which are requested by the Consulate.

1. *Form I-20 properly executed by the school, showing that I have been accepted for a full course of study. The Consulate said that the College has such a form.*
2. *Evidence that I have adequate personal resources or that other arrangements have been made to cover all my expenses in the United States without my resorting to remunerative employment there.*

Please will you be so kind as to furnish me these two documents that I can send them to the Consulate. I am very sorry that you have to wait so long for me. … I am so grateful to you and all the Rotarian families and your friends, because you are all so very kind to me. Now I'm looking forward to your letter and I hope very much that you are not angry about this delay. My parents send to you all good wishes and thanks.

Very sincerely yours, Monika

On the back of this letter is a note in Art Langford's handwriting, saying: "Included is a notarized statement of proof that I will be responsible for your support for a year; I believe it will be satisfactory."

Next is the critical letter from Ventura College that would enable me to obtain the student visa. It was sent by airmail on vellum paper:

Dear Miss Amsler:

Mr. Art Langford and the local Rotary Club have recommended you for admission to Ventura College for this Fall Semester. In order to facilitate your admission routines because of the very short period of time remaining before the opening of school this message will, of necessity, be brief.

An application form is enclosed. Please complete and forward with a statement of recommendation from Dr. Tobler, the principal of your high school, or another school official and enclose with the completed admissions tests (see below). We have a copy of your diploma as presented by Mr. Langford. This will suffice for your preparatory school record.

We are forwarding your admissions tests air mail to Dr. Ed Schütz of the Official Tourist Office at Luzern for administration. Please make the necessary arrangements with Dr. Schütz at the earliest moment. Please advise Dr. Schütz to forward the completed tests to us air mail as soon as you have completed them. Enclose your application form and statement of recommendation as suggested above.

You will hear from us by airmail as soon as we have the opportunity to complete the scoring of your admissions tests.

Some dates for the Fall Semester—Classwork for the Fall Semester 1958-59 is scheduled to begin on Wednesday, September 10. Registration counseling will be by appointment August 25 to September 5. Monday through Friday, September 1-5 is registration for all students. Monday, September 8 is Orientation Day for Freshmen. September 9 is Admissions Day holiday.

Ventura College is a publicly supported two-year junior college and so there is no tuition charge; however, students must purchase their own textbooks. Ventura College is accredited by the Western College Association and is approved by the Attorney General for the attendance of non-immigrant students.

A statement of policy relating to the admission of foreign students is attached. I have just had another communication from Mr. Langford. As a result of this discussion, and because of arrangements that have been made through the local Rotary Club relating to your sponsorship, I am attaching a completed I-20 to speed and facilitate your visa routines. This will not change the procedures outlined above.

Please let me know if we can be of further assistance to you.
Very truly yours, R.W. Pax, Dean of Students

Now, when surveying this correspondence, I'm astonished to realize how many people were involved in helping me. Also, I do not remember being stressed out during that August, a time when I was working hard and being occupied with getting my pilot's license.

Finally, here is my last letter to Mr. Langford after this lengthy, convoluted process, to show that my dream of going to America was becoming a reality:

Dear Mr. Langford,
I thank you very much for your letter and your statement for support and your help to get Form I-20 from Ventura College. I have now sent my completed visa application to the American Consulate and I hope that I'll soon be given the visa.

I had some difficulties getting my flight reservation. SAS had no economy class left. Thus, I will travel with Swissair to New York and from there to Los Angeles with United Airlines scheduled to arrive in Los Angeles at 21:15 on September 7.

I hardly can believe that in three weeks I shall be with your family. I'm very happy. I have been very busy last week with completing forms, and then we have now our International Music Festival in Lucerne, and therefore a lot of work in our office. Dr. Schütz was not able to do with me the tests. Thus, I contacted the instructor of the Spanish class that I had taken in night school, and he is willing to meet with me at the Tourist

Office to administer the English proficiency (TOEFL) test. The other forms and statements for Ventura College are ready for mailing. I'm only awaiting the completed test. Now I have to study hard, because on August 24, I have the final exams for my pilot's license. Then I was with the doctor for revaccination against smallpox, so that's in order now, too. I'm very much looking forward to seeing you and Mrs. Langford and Artie.

My parents send their best wishes to you and your family.
Sincerely yours, Monika

As per stamp in my Swiss passport, I received the non-immigrant "F" visa a week later, on August 22, 1958. I don't remember, but I must have been relieved at its timely arrival. Dr. Schütz made me work until noon on Saturday, September 6—and my flight was scheduled to leave Zürich a quarter past 5 o'clock that afternoon. My parents accompanied me to Zürich.

My mother was sad—she knew in her heart that I would not return. The other Amsler relatives who had come to see me off—my father's six siblings who all lived nearby, with most of their spouses plus four cousins—were just amazed at my courage for going off to far-away America! It would be 1971 before I would see them again, except for my cousin, Angela (standing in front of our very tall cousin Ruedi). She came to visit me in New Mexico in 1962. Just like Edward when he left Shanghai, I was excited about my new adventure and impatient to be on my way.

In the next photo, I am the girl on the left waving to my family at Kloten Airport before boarding; they could watch from an observation deck. In contrast to today, the passengers had few carry-on bags. There was no direct transatlantic flight in those days. The Swissair DC-6B made stops in Cologne (Germany), Shannon (Ireland), and at early dawn in Gander (Newfoundland) before reaching New York later in the morning. Near Boston, the pilots let me visit the cockpit and listen in to air traffic control.

The next aircraft—I think it was a United Airlines DC-7—made a stop in Chicago, where the pilots let me see the cockpit and then escorted me to the waiting area, to the amazement of the other passengers. I slept on and off the rest of the way except for a bumpy approach to Salt Lake City. The plane landed in Los Angeles around 9:15 pm.

Esther Langford, her sister Mae Bell Anderson, and Artie were there to pick me up. We reached the end of my journey—a beautiful adobe ranch home—after midnight, and I was practically asleep on my feet.

The following afternoon, Esther Langford took me to Ventura College to register and buy my textbooks. Two days later, I started college! The next two chapters describe how Edward and I experienced the first semester in what to us was an alien environment before meeting, though he was a US citizen. It was a culture shock in rather different ways for both of us!

CHAPTER FIVE

Edward: In College with Ditches, Weeds, the Sheriff and Missiles

After my discharge from the US Air Force, I was back in San Francisco, the one place in the US where I did not feel like a total stranger. However, I no longer had family here. My father had moved to Kansas City. My brother Chuck was in Southern California working on a survey crew for the California Highway Department, and my sister Maria lived with her husband Bob and two children in Long Beach.

Thinking that my high-school friend Hector was still in the Army, I decided to look up the only other person I knew well—Horace. I was hoping I might be able to stay with him for a few days while I got my bearings. I waited until after working hours before knocking on the door of his apartment. Horace gave me a surprised look and then exclaimed, "Come in; welcome; it's good to see you!" After a bit of chitchat, I came right out and asked, "Can you put me up for a few days?" "Of course," he quickly responded—he seemed to have forgotten the incident that had led to our parting more than four years earlier. Or perhaps he wanted me to think he had acted stupidly because he was drunk, not because he was gay.

I started to look for a job in San Francisco, expecting to use the radio operator experience I had gained while in the Air Force. Just before my discharge, I had passed the exams to be an amateur radio operator, and my assigned station call name was K6JAQ. I had already completed three basic math courses at San Francisco City College, and I thought I could continue there for a while, one course at a time. But now I was quickly finding my radio operator training was of no use at all for getting a civilian job.

One evening after a long day of answering ads and interviews, I stopped at a diner on Market Street for a cup of coffee. As I walked in, I saw a man with a girl sitting at the counter. From the back, he looked like Hector, except for a very short haircut. But as soon as I heard his voice, I knew this was my old friend. I walked over to the counter and tapped him on the shoulder. He turned around and recognized me instantly. "Eduardo!"

Both of us were astonished to meet by chance. I learned that the Army had discharged him the previous day, after the two years of duty required of draftees. He introduced me to the girl and then dismissed her—the two of us wanted to talk. Hector and I moved over to a booth, settled in comfortably, and began sharing our experiences.

Hector started, "I'm now living with an older cousin. My aunt Marianna has moved to a little apartment and is doing well. Why don't you go and visit her?" I jotted down her address and did go and see her a few days later. Then Hector confessed, "My time in Korea was okay, but I hate the Army and I'm glad to be out." In my turn I told him, "I'm just hanging around and looking for a job after getting out of the Air Force a week ago, but my ultimate goal is going to college on the GI bill."

The longer we talked, the more I realized that the close friendship Hector and I had shared no longer existed. It wasn't that we argued, but in listening to him I discovered we did not have the same goals. Before we had gone into military service, we had been content to just drift and live each day without much thought about the future.

I still liked Hector, but I no longer desired to be like him. I now wanted to have a wife and family and a college education so that I could get a good-paying, respectable job in pursuit of the American Dream. He just wanted to turn back the clock and erase the two years spent in the Army—to continue life as it had been before he was drafted. I was surprised to see how much I had grown. Freedom for me now meant making good decisions and assuming responsibility, not just for myself, but also for others. By 1966, after I completed my education, I lost track of Hector—the cultural gap had become too wide.

Picking up Family Threads in California

The next day I telephoned Chuck at the hotel in Ventura where he was staying. He told me, "George and Milly will arrive in San Francisco in two days. Can you meet them at the airport and put them up until Maria can fetch them?"

My father's half-brother—my uncle Art—lived in Palo Alto at this time. He had business in San Francisco the day of my younger siblings' arrival and thus could drive me to pick them up. I still remember that hair-raising ride.

We were running late, and he was driving like a maniac with little regard to posted speed limits! Uncle Art was a well-known psychology professor at Stanford University, with a doctorate from Stanford. His wife was educated at one of the prestigious universities on the East Coast. Both had served in Europe during World War Two. Aunt Marion, Uncle Art's wife, said she did not want George and Milly to stay at their house because of the possibility of my siblings carrying a disease and transmitting it to her sons John, David and Peter. It was a legitimate concern, but nonetheless it hurt.

Uncle Art, who occasionally had contributed financial help to our family, insisted on paying for a hotel room for my siblings for a couple of days. It was impossible for them to stay with Horace—he was adamant in his refusal when I asked. Later, I found out that Uncle Art had driven through the night to Seattle to fetch his mother. He rented a small apartment for her in Berkeley, so she could take care of George and Milly for a few weeks until Maria came to San Francisco to pick them up.

During our phone call, Chuck had asked me to visit him in Ventura. Thus, I packed up my bags, said farewell to Horace, and boarded a bus for the 300-mile trip south on Highway 101. I had no idea this move would radically change my life.

Full-time Freshman with Various Jobs

When I arrived by bus in Ventura, Chuck met me at the bus station and took me to his hotel. I had heard that this was a small city with a beautiful beach and pier about a hundred miles north of Los Angeles. That evening, he and I had a long talk. He asked, "Are you planning to go to college on your GI Bill?" Hesitantly I responded, "I want to find a job first; I'm not sure I'm prepared to start college full-time."

Chuck then explained the community college system in California, which was tuition-free, except for the costs of the textbooks. "You can earn an associate degree and then transfer to a four-year college or university when you're ready. Come and live with me here in Ventura—it has a community college. You can start taking classes right away! Hey, with George joining us, the three of us could get a two-bedroom apartment together." This unexpected offer was like a bright door opening for me, and I gladly accepted. George, who had recently graduated from high school in Hong Kong, would be able to start college at the same time.

By mid-September, Chuck, George and I were settled in a cheaply furnished apartment on Simpson Street. I was allowed to register at Ventura Junior College with my GED. However, the counselor, after reviewing my pitiful grade school record and my practically non-existent high school credits, advised, "It would be best if you learned a trade such as auto mechanics or radio repair." At that point I really didn't have a specific idea of what I wanted to study, but I knew I wanted a university degree in a field where I could earn good money. Out of the blue, I blurted out, "I want to be an engineer." The counselor hesitated and then replied, "Well, with your background, the road will be long and hard, but I am not saying it's impossible." However, his body language and tone of voice conveyed, "Trust me, you won't make it." He signed me up for "bone-head" English and my first science class—elementary physics. Even in my wildest dreams I could not foresee where this decision to go into engineering would take me.

Although Chuck had a steady job with the highway department and I worked part-time as an usher in a downtown movie theatre, we were very short on money because we had to support our mother and four siblings still in Hong Kong. Chuck had a ten-year-old Buick which he needed for driving to work. George and I would take the bus to and from school, and I could walk the few blocks to my theatre job. I had bought a nice Ford for which I had paid $100 from my mustering-out pay of $300, but the same weekend had totaled it in an accident with a drunken driver. I had neglected to buy insurance, and this put me in the wrong. It resulted in my having to make sixteen monthly payments to cover $160 in repairs to the other driver's car. Unknown to me, it also got me a suspended license.

It was not until the end of November that payments on the GI Bill were approved (including an allotment for my mother), and I started to get a regular monthly check. For several days we subsisted on a bit of cabbage and a large box of wheat germ which we ate raw, fried, or boiled. Fortunately, we were still close enough to our wartime past that one meal a day was something we could deal with. Another weekend we had boiled rice with soy sauce and oil—a tasty dish!

In later years, I would brag about making it through college with little prior education. But in reality, it took a tremendous effort in the beginning to pass my courses and overcome my ignorance. For example, most of the other students had physics in high school and thus were familiar with the words, concepts and phenomena that were being discussed, but which were new to me. I was only able to work an exam problem in mechanics after I asked the instructor to explain what a *cam* was. But most of the time, I felt truly lost.

What saved me were the lab experiments and my experience on the Danish ship and in the Air Force. These enabled me to relate this new academic knowledge to real life—such as how levers can multiply an applied force. Initially, principles like Newton's law of gravity totally baffled me. In the end, the challenge of wanting to succeed against the odds helped me to persevere, and I managed to get a good grade in this course. But the more I learned, the more fascinating science became, and I started to get top grades. My natural aptitude for math and its practical applications, which far exceeded my other skills, made math courses easy and fun.

Science and higher math mesmerized me, and I became a full-fledged agnostic. Religion as a whole had little influence on my life as I grew into adulthood. If God was out there somewhere, He couldn't be known and was thus irrelevant. It seemed to me that everything was a gamble, and life was determined by probability. For example, the miracles in the Bible I had heard about in grammar school were simply events that occurred with very low probability but nevertheless happened. Life to me was like a *mahjong* game. Each player is dealt a hand of thirteen tiles, and each player skillfully tries to better his or her hand—by discarding unwanted tiles, one at a time—on a road of continuous improvement, until one of the four players in the game reaches an acceptable winning hand and time runs out. Care was required: discarding the wrong tile could spell disaster. For the next few years, I believed I could improve my life and economic status through education. Events that were beyond my control were determined by luck, fate, or probability. Life meant uncertainty and change, and continuous adjustments were necessary to make the best of each situation.

What I needed right now was part-time work. I had a couple of classes with Bill Winchell, and we had become friends. He was muscular and had a job digging ditches for a contractor who built brick walls and fences around Ventura County. The hourly wages were phenomenal, about three times what I earned as an usher. Bill invited me to join him, and I jumped at the chance. We were paid by the foot. But since Bill worked twice as fast as I did, we soon decided that he would get two-thirds of the pay. He picked me up in his old car, and we worked mostly after classes, unless we had a rush job. I was unaware how dangerous it was to ride in Bill's car. He put water into the brake cylinders because oil was too expensive. I thought this was a smart idea, not realizing that the brakes could fail catastrophically sooner or later through rust build-up in the cylinders.

One Sunday, after we had worked for several hours and had made good progress on a ditch, an old lady in a housecoat suddenly appeared, wielding a broom and yelling, "Why aren't you boys in church?" We did not see the broom as a weapon; she probably was doing some house cleaning. Still, we were taken aback. Off-hand we couldn't think of a pithy answer, like asking her why she wasn't in church. Since we didn't want to create a scene in the neighborhood, we decided the best action was to take our lunch break early. Thus, we beat a hasty retreat.

Although the pay for ditch digging was good, it was irregular. I told Bill, "I need to have a steadier income." He suggested, "Go and talk to my father. He is a gardener and is always looking for help, especially with weeding." Bill made it sound like any idiot would know how to weed. In all of my previous life, I had never been around plants, but I was too embarrassed to own up to my ignorance. Nonetheless, I took the job.

The next afternoon, Bill dropped me off outside a large office complex surrounded by an ivy-covered slope. He said, "I'll be back in two hours to pick you up." I thought weeding meant to pull out everything—which I proceeded to do on one side of the building. When Bill returned, he was really upset: "I can't understand why you had to clear the entire bed." We then replanted as much of the ivy as best we could. Back at his house, I was embarrassed to take the money for the work. The next day, Bill's father told me, "Sorry, I don't need you anymore."

The Administration Office at Ventura College had occasional job postings. I was given a number at the Sheriff's Office to call—the county sheriff was campaigning for re-election and needed a driver. Every afternoon I drove around the Ojai and Simi valleys with him sitting next to me in a truck which carried a large billboard in the back. He told me where to drive and toot the horn every time we saw potential voters. The sheriff was grumpy and didn't say much beyond complaining that I was driving too slowly on curvy roads. However, as soon as we came into a town, he would greet people with a big smile. Neither of us knew during the days I was driving him around, that I had a suspended driver's license as a result of my earlier accident. The sheriff did win the election.

The following week, I saw an advertisement in the newspaper for data reduction technicians with Land-Air Corporation at Point Mugu, south of Ventura. I went for an interview and was offered the job, starting immediately. Chuck and I bought a used brown Volkswagen so I could get to work. I obtained insurance through assigned risk, and my driver's license was reinstated. I was put on the graveyard shift—from midnight to 8 am. Students with some seniority were on the swing shift, and the day shift was for regular employees.

We had to reduce the data that came from missiles (such as the Sparrow) fired from aircraft. We calculated the motion, velocity, and acceleration and then passed the results to the engineers. Even with mechanical calculators to do number crunching, it was a tedious process. Many college students were doing this work, with much turnover. I asked my supervisor to consider my brother George for a job, and George was hired.

It took a while for my body to adjust to working all night, going to school all morning, sleeping a few hours in the afternoon, and doing homework before going to work again at midnight. Consequently, I was always tired and had zero social life. I had to use every hour on weekends for studying unless I was training in the Air Force Reserve as a non-commissioned officer. This training every other Saturday afternoon or evening was enjoyable, and it meant additional income.

One afternoon, Chuck and George went out. Somehow the gas was turned on in the apartment's old heater without having been lit with a match—there was no automatic igniter or shut-off valve. Despite my utter exhaustion, the putrid smell of the gas woke me up. Since my brothers did not return home for hours, I would have been dead if the odor had not roused me. I attributed my escape to luck.

Living with Chuck was not easy. He was a neat freak and moody. I felt he treated me as the little kid that had followed him around in Shanghai and took orders from him. But now I was working and studying full-time—I simply did not have the energy to always put everything away. His criticism and bossiness would not have bothered me if I had been under less stress. George, on the other hand, was so happy to be in the US, he just did what Chuck told him to do. He had a quiet, easy-going temperament, and he likely found living with his grown-up brothers better than coping with five younger siblings, as he had done in Hong Kong. However, out of Chuck's earshot, we soon took to calling him the "quacker duck."

Early during the spring term at Ventura College, Land-Air Corporation needed four new programmers at our worksite. All data reduction technicians and supervisors could take the test, which was mostly about math aptitude. The top four people from the list would be interviewed for the programming jobs. I had the top score, two points above Uve Ibbs, one of Ventura College's math whiz kids. My brother George and another student from Ventura College, Chris Purcell, were also in the top group. Ultimately, George ended up working as a programmer for Land-Air Corporation at Vandenberg Air Force Base until his retirement.

To be hired as programmers, we needed to have a secret clearance. It took less than two months to clear the other three, including my brother. But I did not receive a clearance, and the investigation dragged on for months. It finally dawned on me that the reason was not my background in China or my relatives still living there, but the suspicion that I might be a homosexual. Chris mentioned the questions the FBI asked him about me were about my character and suspected homosexual acts and had nothing to do with my growing up in China.

Staying with Horace even for a short while after my separation from active military service (and using his address as the forwarding address for my mail) had been a big mistake. It confirmed in their minds that we must have had an improper relationship—they assumed guilt by association without any other evidence. Because I did not get a secret clearance, the door to my becoming a military pilot was now shut for good. In fact, I was still under investigation until I left Land-Air.

To get the maximum benefits under the GI Bill, I had to take a full academic load each semester. Thus, for the spring term of 1959, I signed up for mechanical drawing, English composition, elementary chemistry, the first calculus course, and the required physical education. Two of these courses turned out to be "winning" tiles in my *mahjong* game of life, although I did not know this at the time.

Except for math, I still found it very difficult to keep up with my classmates who had a high school education and did not have to work full time. I felt inferior academically, in looks, origin, and economic background, and I didn't think I could compete with them on a social level. However, deep down I did have my antennas out for someone I might be able to woo as my wife. I had no idea how soon this would happen!

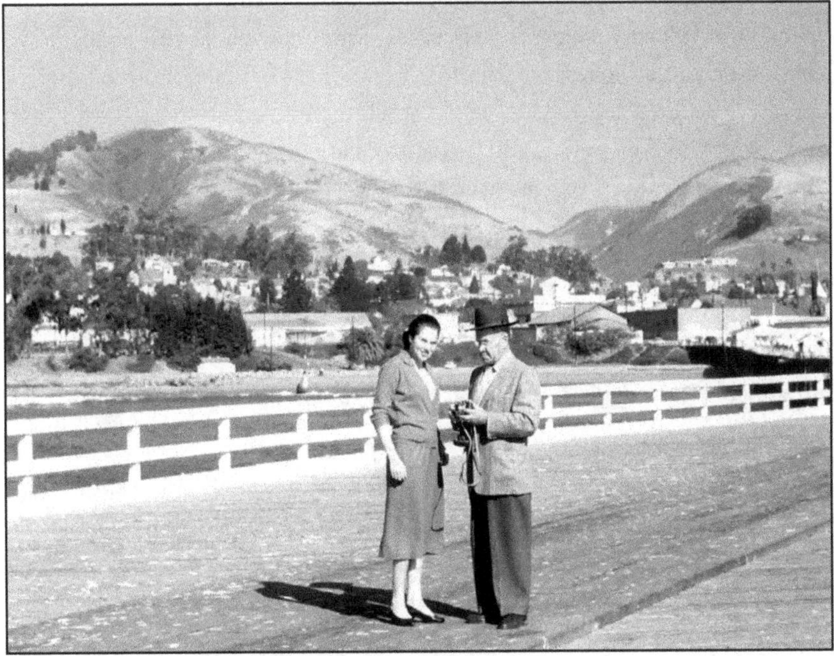

The photo shows the pier at Ventura beach and the foothills in late 1958, with Monika standing next to Art Langford's father. The following spring, she was to see them from above while piloting a small airplane, as she will recount in the following chapter.

CHAPTER SIX

Monika: In College with Apples, a Pool, Strange Customs and a Pilot's License

The Langford family lived on Rancho Arnaz, halfway between Ventura and Ojai. This ranch was a large apple orchard with a cider mill and a roadside barn with an open-front store. Their one-story adobe home was originally built by Native Americans about a hundred years earlier, before California became part of the United States. It was shaded by live oaks and palms, and it had a beautiful fenced-in swimming pool with view of the surrounding hills covered with brown grass. The Ventura River, full of boulders, bisected the valley. I could smell the eucalyptus trees nearby, and later there would be orange and lemon trees in bloom—a heavenly fragrance bringing memories of Italian vacations to this girl from the north side of the Alps.

Here, translated into English, is an excerpt from the letter I wrote to my parents on my first morning in California, typed on an old machine with an American keyboard, which surprised me, as the letters were arranged in an unfamiliar pattern, and the German vowels ä, ö, ü were missing.

Liebes Mameli, lieber Papi,

I'm writing only briefly, so that you can see that I arrived safely. The trip was very nice, but at the end I was very tired. … Oh, here it is soooooo hot, I'm already all sweaty just from getting up this morning. But everything is very beautiful. The home on the inside looks like a blockhouse. But overall, it is just as I had imagined America, with so much space everywhere. The Langfords are very nice to me. Now I have to hurry, because we have to go to the school to get me registered. My English is such that I understand about half of what is spoken, but it's going all right otherwise. I should have brought more clothes for hot weather. Got to stop, it's already 11 o'clock. We're going to look at Ventura. Last night I only saw the lights.

In my second letter two days later, I described in more detail my first impressions and experiences:

Now my first party is already behind me. Yesterday, Artie invited about a dozen of her girlfriends. There was a buffet with turkey. Here, they have some strange things to eat, with the meat and jam, sweet and sour, all mixed up. Corn, cooked like yellow peas or simply on the cob, or Lima beans which are like very large peas. For breakfast there are oranges, or corn flakes or baked bacon with jam and pineapple juice or apple juice or chocolate, and raspberries. For lunch yesterday we were at Mrs. Langford's club, the Soroptimists. Salads here have weird dressings. Normally, lunch would be a sandwich.

Mami, you should see the stove in the Langford's kitchen. One can program each burner for how long it should be on. Unbelievably complicated! And there is a washing machine and clothes dryer. But the best thing is the large swimming pool out on the patio.

The ranch is about 10 minutes by car from Ventura on a winding road. It is great how wide the roads are here. Already the first morning, Artie took me into town. I could bathe my feet in the Pacific. Then we visited her grandparents, aunt, and boyfriend, as well as some other people. One simply walks into these homes without knocking, just calls out "hi" and makes oneself comfortable. Most people have at least one car, and many have two but no garage. The cars are parked in front of the house. All houses are single family homes and far apart. One can't get anywhere on foot. I'll have to take the school bus to get to college.

One has to set aside an hour to eat lunch around noon in the class schedule, and there is time to do homework, since the bus won't leave until 4 p.m. And in the evening, when one is tired, one can watch television. There are two dogs, a boxer named Flash and a brown miniature poodle named Suzie. I've already been at the bank to open a savings account with my $150. Today, there will be an article about me in the local newspaper.

On the way to Ventura, there is first a small village, Casitas Springs, and then an oil field with many drilling rigs. There are many palm trees here, as well as eucalyptus trees, and many others that I have never seen before, also fig trees and citrus and avocados, and so many beautiful flowers. Mr. Langford has 18 kinds of apples, and right now is the harvest. There are many Mexican workers who pick the apples. Otherwise I'm still a bit tired from my trip, even though I slept until 10 o'clock this morning. It is so hot here. It is a bit cooler in Ventura because of the ocean. Next Sunday we have to go to Los Angeles and then Whittier, because Artie has to go to school there.

Two days later I wrote about my weekly class schedule, which included two evenings of aviation ground school. I mentioned that the textbooks for my classes were terribly expensive. For example, for psychology the cost was $6.60 which the Rotary Club was paying. It took me one hour to get to school on the bus, leaving at 7 am. Artie gave me a stack of summer clothes that were too small for her, and they fit me well. And I still felt like I was in a dream. Then in my next letter, I mentioned a visit to Mrs. Langford's sister, where I made a Swiss salad with Boston lettuce and a simple vinaigrette dressing, because I found that the American salad dressings were simply awful. The family, including the three boys Allen 14, Jimmy 12 and Davie 9, liked my salad a lot.

Soon, I was able to report to my parents that I had a perfect score on the first algebra test but had some trouble in history. Spanish was easy since I'd had an introductory adult education class in Switzerland in night school. The English class for international students was a lot of fun with boys from Iran, Hong Kong, Shanghai, and a Hawaiian from Honolulu, and girls from Peru (Zora), Ecuador, Colombia, France (Jeanette), and Mexico (Lucia).

I wrote that "one has to pay attention like the devil not to miss anything important during the lectures and take good notes." This was hard for me at the beginning until I became proficient in English. I complained that I had mountains of homework in all my subjects. But then I discovered I could get an A or B on a test even without studying—being graded on a curve was a new experience—I didn't need to get stressed out like I had been in high school when preparing for exams.

One evening I was at the Rotary Club and had to give a speech. Next, I was sent to attend a three-day conference at the Beverly Hills YMCA Camp Wakonda near Malibu as a representative for Ventura College. I was one of twelve students of which four were foreign students. The various discussion sessions were fascinating and an eye opener: I was amazed to discover that Americans can actually think!

How did I take the aviation evening class without inconveniencing the Langfords too much? I could walk to Mrs. Anderson's house and eat supper there. Then Mrs. Langford would pick me up and take me back to the college campus, where she was taking a class in photography. This way we could drive home together after our classes. By the way, my English test for college admission that I took in Switzerland was almost as good as that of the average American student. It was incredible to me how few of the young Americans knew correct English, and many had trouble with spelling.

A new experience for me was riding a yellow school bus to the high school in Ventura, where I switched to another bus for the Ventura Junior College campus. I did this until I found rides in cars with other students for most mornings. Another challenge was physical education. I did okay in basketball and volleyball, but softball completely baffled me; I had never seen a bat or glove before, and of course the rules were unfamiliar.

Art Langford won many awards for his apple cider (see snapshot). There is a cultural aspect on how I perceived the Langfords that astonished me. In Switzerland, educated white collar people looked down on farmers, who were considered low-class and uncouth, or smelly if they were mucking around with cattle! Now it dawned on me that here was this family I came to admire and respect very much. They were not at all like the stereotypical Swiss farmers. Esther had a college degree in home making and Art in agriculture. Their knowledge of world affairs and interest in international relations was astonishing, from the books they read to the organizations they supported. They were broad-minded, and their friends came from many walks of life. They were *farmers* and way above my family in their education and worldview! They helped me see the world and people in a less judgmental way.

I also learned to appreciate the difficulties of being a farmer. For example, a scary time at Rancho Arnaz came in mid-October, when a forest fire burned for days about eight miles away. Ash and cinders rained down, and the water in the swimming pool turned black.

Because of safety and liability rules, I was discouraged from apple picking (there were Mexican laborers hired for that). Also, the male employees at the barn store did not want me to even carry empty crates around. The only job I could do was to search and pick out rotten apples in the boxes and crates.

This photo shows the roadside barn where the Langfords sold their apples and cider. To the left, the highway continues north toward Ojai. Today, this historic property houses horse stables and a Girl Scout camp.

I did help some with house cleaning and doing the dishes, but in general, I think I was rather spoiled by Mrs. Langford. I did take Flash the boxer for walks into the hills occasionally, where he would pick up ticks, which had to be carefully removed with tweezers.

Although I was originally under the impression that I would have to move to other Rotary families, Mrs. Langford said there was no hurry about this. I think she missed having her daughter at home and was glad for my companionship. She wanted her only daughter to attend college away from home to become independent and more responsible. I had her bedroom all to myself during the week. Artie often came home on weekends when she

could get a ride for the five-hour drive. I enjoyed being with the friendly Langford family (which included Art's parents and Esther's sister Mae Bell Anderson). However, I had trouble understanding Artie (who was a temperamental redhead) being disrespectful to her parents. The photo on the previous page shows Artie and me in front of a huge hedge of poinsettias blooming at Christmas.

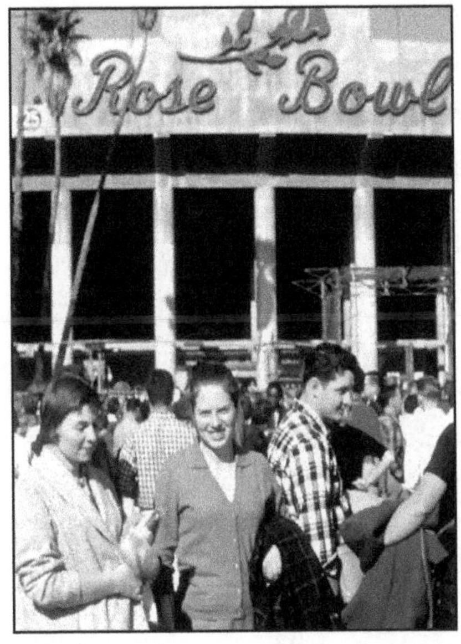

Art and Esther Langford took us girls to see the Rose Parade and the Rose Bowl Game in Pasadena on New Year's Day. In the photo, Artie is standing to my right. But American football seemed astoundingly violent to me since I was used to European soccer.

Having access to the refrigerator for a snack was a new freedom—this was not allowed in my home in Switzerland. I gained twenty pounds during the first year I lived in Ventura, helping myself to peanut butter or ice cream for a snack when I got off the bus in the afternoon. I was glad to be able to swim in the Langford's pool almost every day for exercise and to cool off during the hot fall weather. And I delighted in tasting all eighteen kinds of apples, eating at least four or five every day.

Then it was soon time to sign up for the next term's classes: mechanical drawing, plane geometry, intermediate algebra, more Spanish, and more English for foreign students, as well as social dance. I was keenly interested in mechanical drawing, a subject only open to boys in Switzerland.

Mrs. Langford had become concerned that I did not go to school dances nor had other dates. I suspect they asked George who helped on their ranch to take me to a school dance. I sewed a new dress, and Mrs. Langford bought me a pair of shoes and a little matching purse. I had trouble finding a shoe that fit, as Americans seem to have much narrower feet than mine. Mrs. Langford also lent me her black shawl, so I had a very pretty ensemble. I don't remember anything about this date, except that we went out for a meal before the dance where we had root beer. I tasted it suspiciously, thinking it was the alcoholic kind of beer. But the school dance and the dancing class were disasters for me. Being klutzy and inexperienced, I stepped on many of my partners' toes.

Later, when a Korean student in my English class gave me a makeup kit, and an Arab student wanted to take me on a date to a restaurant far out in the country, the Langfords advised me against pursuing a relationship with those guys. There was also a fellow who wanted to take me to a play in Los Angeles, but he was very fat. I politely declined.

I am glad that Art and Esther Langford watched out for me—they felt responsible for me in *loco parentis*. They asked me to get permission from my father to continue flying. I had just passed the test for the American pilot's license (good for one year) with a score of 100%, and I was now ready to do some flying out of the Oxnard airport.

Reading my old letters makes me feel like I am watching a person I had known more than half a century ago and then had mostly forgotten. I am appalled to see how arrogant I was. I do not remember praying during those days; I was too busy adjusting to the new American culture and enjoying this adventure. Neither Edward nor I had an inkling of what was going to happen on the first day of class in January 1959, the start of the spring semester at Ventura College.

PART TWO

Marriage, Education, and Becoming Parents 1959-1969

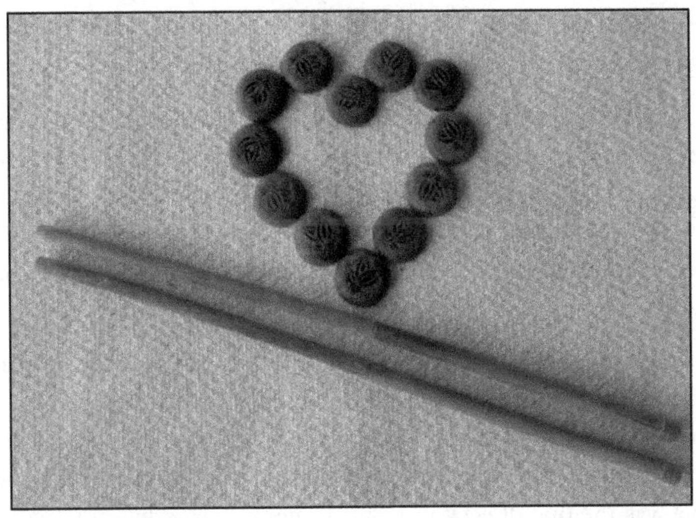

8 September 2019

My dear Grandchildren:

Are you ready to hear how I met your Grandmama Monika and what happened next? It was not love at first sight—quite the contrary. It just goes to show you that God works in mysterious ways.

So, enjoy the story. Maybe the one lesson here—true for the rest of our lives—was to give love time to grow. As you will see from our continuing story, there was much joy, much work, much learning, and much patience needed. And then there were the unexpected and special gifts that came along. Here, in Part Two, I'm telling the story, but Monika has added comments and details in all but two chapters, and she wrote Chapter 14. Also, she selected and inserted the photos, formatted the postscript, and wrote the appendices. And she did numerous rounds of editing and of course all the word processing, a final labor of love.

With much love from your Yehyeh

CHAPTER SEVEN

Edward: Courting a Swiss Woman

The first day of spring term, my life was about to take another unexpected turn. The campus of Ventura Junior College consisted mainly of bungalows for classrooms connected by shaded walkways. The moment I was approaching the door to the classroom for mechanical drawing, I noticed a very pretty woman walking towards me, and she turned to the same door.

I wanted to start a conversation with her and was about to say something trite like, "What's a nice girl like you doing in a place like this?" when I blurted out, "You will be the only girl in this class." She smiled. She confessed later that she almost replied, "Of course—what a dumb thing to say." She chose a seat in the front row, and I found a place in the back, near my brother George.

About three weeks later, this same woman was transferred into my English composition class. She had been doing so well in the special section for foreign students—George was a student in that class, too—that the instructor felt she was ready for a regular class. It so happened the only seat available was the one directly in front of me. During a lull in a lecture, she turned around, looked at me, and whispered shyly, "I didn't know you were George's brother." I thought that was a rather stupid thing to say.

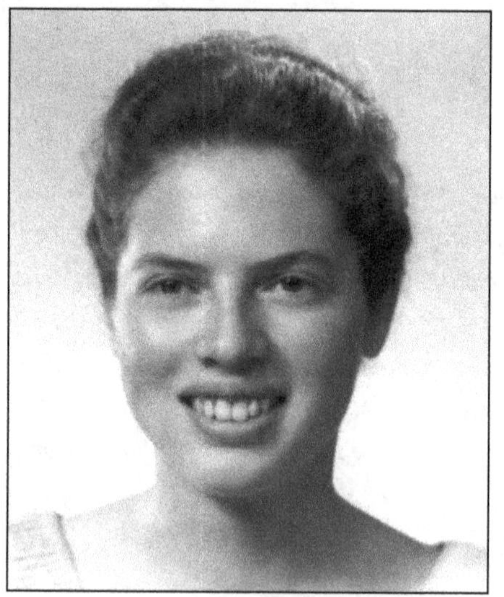

It didn't take long before I became very interested in this woman. I asked my brother to tell me everything he knew about her. "She seems to have a boyfriend who brings her to school in his car." This didn't sound good. I perked up when he continued, "By the way, she is a pilot and a top student." I started to watch her in the cafeteria. I observed that she brought a sandwich and would merely buy a drink, whereas her friends would get a full tray of food for lunch. I concluded she was very frugal. After only a few weeks I decided she had all the qualities I wanted in a wife. Now I had to develop a strategy on how best to pursue her.

Since she took the bus to go home from school three days each week, my first approach was not to ask for a date, which she might decline. Instead, I thought it less risky to tell her, "I'm going to take you home in my car." To my delight she agreed. I later found out she had no romantic interest in the fellow who drove her to the college; this was just a matter of convenience. She couldn't believe a "tall, dark, and handsome" guy like me would pay attention to her. She had not been popular with boys during her school years, and thus she overlooked that I *told* her I would take her home instead of *asking*.

She lived with a Rotary family on an apple ranch halfway between Ventura and Ojai, and it took a while to get there on a winding road. After a couple of times, I decided to make my move. I invited her for a walk in the orchard, and we ended up sitting on a large tree trunk. I wrapped my arms around her and kissed her. Since she seemed to enjoy my embrace, I began to feel more confident and relaxed. Only much later did I learn how close I was to disaster at that moment. She had never been kissed romantically before and she looked straight in my face while I had my eyes closed. She almost burst out laughing, as this struck her as very funny. Whenever I had some spare time in the next weeks, we spent it on that log.

I was sure this woman was everything I wanted in a wife: beautiful, intelligent (especially in math), and frugal. Her love for flying attracted me as well. I developed a great admiration for this Monika Amsler—no one else had ever stood so high in my esteem. I was impressed that the subject of her English term paper was the X-15, an experimental airplane. I started to think about her day and night. I got behind in my studying and had to drop my chemistry class, thus losing a portion of my GI Bill stipend. But since I had a full-time job with Land-Air Corporation at Point Mugu, this was not much of a hardship. I was still able to send my mother the monthly support payment at the level she expected.

I was also in danger of dismally failing mechanical drawing. Precise drawing, as opposed to cartooning, was excruciating for me and took a lot of effort and concentration. I was in great fear of someone taking Monika from me, because I previously had that experience with other women. She had a real talent for technical drawing and loved the course. I enlisted her help with the final design project, not just because I was in trouble in the class, but also to keep her close to me. With her patient coaching, I was able to raise my grade to passing.

Monika had signed up for mechanical drawing as well as geometry and algebra because she could not take higher math or technical courses in the commercial high school for girls that she had attended. On our study dates, I learned she grew up in Switzerland. Her father was a chief engineer for hydraulic turbines with Bell Machine Works in Kriens, and her mother was from the French-speaking part of Switzerland—knowing how to speak French was another thing we had in common. I also found out she had a younger sister.

I had a sense that Monika was running away from something, although she appeared composed and seemed to have her life together, unlike me. Later, I would find out her father was strict and domineering. She was not keen on returning to Switzerland—she delighted in the freedom and opportunities she found in America, especially for women. That was fortunate for me. I felt from the way she began to look at me that she was falling in love with me, and during a tender moment I did say the words, "I love you, too."

Being a gambler, I boldly told her to marry me after only a few dates. To my surprise she said, "Yes, I will—if you will remove all photos of past girlfriends from your wallet and album, and if you have a bank account." That was her frugal Swiss upbringing. I agreed to both terms. That I was able to meet the second condition was an incredible coincidence: I had opened a savings account at the Bank of America only the week before with a deposit of one dollar. Monika didn't ask how much I had in it. Marriage to Monika turned out to be the *Mega Jackpot* in my life. I counted myself lucky I had not married Bettie, Nonie, or Esther (see my first book for the sad details).

I discussed our marriage plans with her "surrogate father," Mr. Langford, who felt responsible for her welfare. Neither Art nor Esther Langford voiced any objections, but in the climate of that day, Esther recommended we should live in Hawaii because our children would be Eurasian and might not be accepted on the mainland. I felt that, although well meaning, she must be a racist. All the feelings of inferiority about being biracial washed over me again. I did expect that my children would have predominantly Caucasian rather than Chinese features, since I was half-Chinese. On the whole, this turned out to be the case, but they still suffered a fair amount of teasing and discomfort at school because they were "different." Monika could not imagine there would be any problems whatsoever, having grown up in a homogeneous society and then making friends in the US with international students from many countries and ethnic groups.

I wanted us to get married as soon as possible, but there was a hindrance. Because Monika was on a student visa, she had to be in the US for a whole year before she could marry. She had to renew her visa, even though we set September 8 (the day after the year was up) as our wedding day. Our instructor in the mechanical drawing class and his wife (Ralph and Natalie Sylvester) were kind and willing to sponsor Monika for the second year.

Since the Langfords were traveling extensively during that summer, Monika lived with friends of theirs who had a small house on top of the hill behind Ventura. Ray York worked at Point Mugu, and Peggy was the director of the regional Girl Scouts. In exchange for room and board, Monika babysat Ray's daughter Julie. She took trigonometry and college algebra, and I gave her a ride to and from campus where I was taking the chemistry class I had previously dropped. Ray had been stationed in Chunking during World War II, and we both worked at Point Mugu, so I had a closer rapport with him than I did with the Langfords. Monika chose Peggy as her matron of honor for our wedding.

The arrangement with the Yorks turned out to be a perfect solution for all. During a recent telephone call, Peggy still remembered how glad she was to have found Monika to babysit, and the Langfords had a reliable host family for Monika to take their place. Peggy and Esther had labored together in scouting for many years. Of course, Monika and I were thrilled that she had such a pleasant place to stay, with room and board included. Here is a photo of Ray York with one of his "birds" (drones) during an open house at Point Mugu.

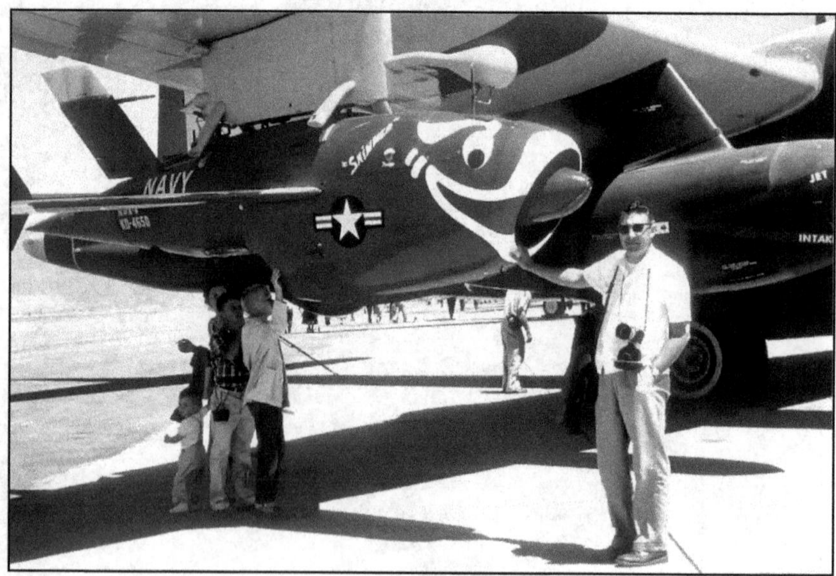

In June, since I was in the Air Force Reserve, I had to attend a two-week training course at Madera Air Force Base. During that time, I called Monika once on the telephone and wrote three brief love letters—I've never been much for writing. She wrote longer, chatty letters to me in green ink. I'm glad she kept these letters; they help us remember the brief time of our courtship. With minor deletions, here are these letters.

6/15/1959

My Dearest Monika,

Started to write you a letter last night when I arrived, but felt exhausted before I could finish the letter, so I just left it till tonight.

I arrived about 9:00 p.m. last night and just as I have predicted this is merely a small radar site. Although the place is small, it has quite a few recreational facilities such as a small but beautiful swimming pool, a recreational hall and a tiny theatre. I was at the swimming pool for quite a few hours today just lying on the grass, swimming a little and thinking of you. It's real quiet at night here, except for the crickets chirping a little. It is an ideal place for some rest, although I have to work 8 hours. It's only been two days since I last saw you and I have already begun to miss you.

Take good care of yourself, be good, and I love you, Edward.

A few days later, I got some mail at the base. It was addressed to: A/1C Edward Lumsdaine, AF 19517840, 774th AC&W Squadron (ADC) Madera AFS, California.

Ventura, June 17, 1959

Dearest Edward,

How are you? I've been thinking of you all the time, what you might be doing up there. Ray and Peggy York and Julie keep me fairly busy; imagine I was fixing hamburgers for supper today. I am tired now, because I went to Oxnard to take the written examination for the commercial pilot's license. I was there at 7:30, but it started only at nine o'clock. It was supposed to take five hours, but I did it in four hours. There were a lot of things I didn't know. So many questions were on radio, on tower frequencies and so on; I was completely lost. The questions on air traffic rules I didn't like either. I only hope I get 70% out of it. I'll know it in about 10 days. After the test I went flying, first 45 minutes dual, and then 35 minutes solo. That was nice. The instructor promised me, if I didn't wait too long to the next time, that he'll give me just a check ride, and then I can fly with you.

Last Sunday I cooked spaghetti. Then I wrote the letter to my mother. She'll get it sometimes this week. Oh, I wish you were here; I miss you so much. I love you. Are you going to write to me soon? Is it very hot weather where you are? Here it is terribly hot. Every time I look out to the ocean, I think of you. I look out to the ocean very often.

Forever yours, Monika

Ventura, June 18, 1959

My dearest Edward,

Thank you so much for calling me today. I was so happy to hear from you. I got a little sunburned today, because we went down to the beach this afternoon. In the morning I was baking some peanut butter cookies. They were very tasty, but it took me almost three hours to make them. Peggy wasn't here, so I had to hunt alone all around the kitchen for the different things to put in. First, I had to translate the recipe more or less. Oh well, it was fun, and I'm getting used to it. I'm just a little bit tired now.

Next Friday, Peggy and Ray are taking me to Oxnard to see the play "Cat on a Hot Tin Roof." I'm always thinking of you, what you might do all day. What kind of work do you have there? I'm longing for you. I wish you were here. The days are so long without you.

Love, Monika

Ventura, June 18, 1959

My dear Edward,

I promised to write you. I felt tired this evening. I was so busy all day. I cooked and sewed and watched the children, and after dinner Peggy took me downtown because I had to buy some stationary. But it was pay-day, too. Peggy gave me five dollars; this'll give me my trigonometry textbook. Today I almost couldn't see the ocean, it was so foggy and it was cool, too. Just one little question: Did you quit smoking yet?

Are you writing to me again? You know, I'm waiting for the mail every day, it comes around two o'clock. I'm so sorry that my letters take such a long time to reach you. Oh, I don't know why I have to think of you all the time. Only eight days and I'll see you again. You be good, too, now. My thoughts are with you always.

I love you, Monika

20 June 1959

My Very Dearest Monika,

I was very disappointed that I couldn't come to Ventura and see you this weekend; this last week has passed very slow for me and I missed you. Had a wonderful dream last night. I dreamed that I was with you, and it was wonderful to see your smiling face again.

The heat here is really quite terrible, the thermometer hit 107 deg today and it was really hot, it is almost as bad as being out in the desert.

I have a little room of my own here on the base and I have been doing quite a bit of reading (six Western paperbacks) because it is very quiet here, especially at night, and I don't want to go to a bar off base.

Will write again on Monday, in the meantime think of me as I do of you, take care, and I love you, Edward

21 June 1959

My Dearest Monika,

Both your letters arrived here yesterday morning, and I was very happy to receive them (anxious too). I was also very happy to hear that you have written to your mother about us, I hope she will give her consent to our marriage. Don't worry about the test. I have complete confidence in you, and I am quite sure that you will obtain the necessary score; first chance we get we will go flying. (I am not a good pilot, but I will offer my services as radio operator.)

It's Sunday today and I am off from work. I was at the swimming pool most of the day just taking life easy, although I regret spending so much time there because my back and legs are slightly sunburned; it's starting to hurt a little. The rest of today I spent washing and ironing my clothes. We have a washing and drying machine here so it is quite convenient.

You know, so many things remind me of you. I find myself thinking of you almost all day long, wishing I was with you right now. I can hardly wait till Saturday to see you again, so until then take care and keep smiling. I love you so very much.

Yours always, Edward

Ventura, June 22, 1959

My dearest Edward,

I am so happy to get your letter today; thank you. The days, and the nights, too, just don't seem to pass, do they? I feel so sorry for you, with all this heat you have up there. It's foggy around here, and cool. Yesterday, we couldn't even see Main Street from the hill. Next Thursday noon, Peggy, Julie and I are leaving for Hearst Castle on Highway One. I guess it'll be a nice trip. We'll be back Friday afternoon.

I am so glad that you come home next Friday and that you don't have to stay until the 29th. How did you manage that? You should see the kids; Julie is seven and the neighbors' Chris is six and little Julie is two. What they do all day long! Yesterday they got hold of a bottle of liquid soap; they spilled it all over the patio. It took me half an hour to get all that soap off. Or they try to cook and really make a mess in the kitchen.

Oops, I've to get ready now, and get Julie ready, too. She has to get her hair cut. We have to walk down to Peggy's office. Good-bye. You know, I'm carrying your letters around all the time. It's the only thing I have from you. I love you, Edward, only you.

Love, Monika

Ventura, June 22, 1959

My dearest Edward,

Tomorrow I'll be ironing. I don't mind, the time passes faster, and I can listen to some records, like our "Sleeping Beauty" waltz. Today I was just writing a little, making some lace, and looking after the kids. Mr. York just came home; it's already half past eight, but they launched something important at Point Mugu, that's why he was late. Then I got a phone call from Mrs. Knecht, a Swiss. She invited me (and you too) to a Swiss party. It's a dinner, Saturday at six o'clock. She said we could leave afterwards if we planned to do something else. You know, the only thing that really counts for me is that you'll be back and that I'll see you Saturday, and we'll be together. I love you, and I was missing you so much. It will be so wonderful, the next weekend with you, and the next week, and all the time we'll have together, the next year, and all the following years.

Peggy told me it was all right with her if I went to the Swiss party. At the party, there would be about eight to ten people, all Swiss, but mostly elderly people. These parties are quite nice; I have been at two of them, and this one would be my last one. Just call me what you would like to do, and I'll phone them Saturday if we aren't going, OK?

Only four days more and you'll be here, and everything will be all right. I think of you, all the time. I love you; I love only you, I'm sure. Be careful now, and have a nice trip home.

Love, Monika

The Swiss party turned out to be great. I loved both the Swiss onion pies (a type of quiche) and the open-face Swiss apple pies with custard. It's interesting that Monika and I recollect the food but not what we did the rest of the evening.

Below is the hand-written letter I wrote to Monika's father in Switzerland to assure him that I had a full-time job and was able to support a wife. Monika found it among his belongings after he died. He had numbered all her letters she wrote to her parents from America, and this one was #46.

July 16, 1959

Dear Mr. and Mrs. Amsler,

It has been quite some time since I first thought of writing a letter to both of you, but somehow, I couldn't organize my thoughts well enough to express the exact purpose of writing such a letter. Now, however, I am sorry that I didn't, mainly because I am engaged to your daughter without requesting permission from you. I have been very inconsiderate, please accept my sincere apology. Although Monika and I grew up in a different type of environment and the fact that we have different family backgrounds, we are not in the least bit influenced by this. We accept each other as individuals, and of course I am very much in love with her.

I was born in Hong Kong, China, on September 30, 1937. At the age of three, my family moved to Shanghai, China where I lived till the age of fifteen, at which time I left to come to the United States. My father is a Scottish-American; my mother is Chinese.

After I arrived in the United States, I attended Galileo High School in San Francisco till the age of seventeen when I enlisted in the Air Force for four years. After my discharge from the Air Force on August 15, 1958, I came here to Ventura to live with my two brothers and to continue my college education.

At the present time I am attending Ventura College on the Veteran GI Bill which finances me through college, and I also work at night from midnight till 8 am. As a technician for Land-Air Corp at Pacific Missile Range, Point Mugu, Calif. When I get off work in the morning. I go directly to school. My major in school is in the field of general engineering.

I am sure there are questions in your mind which might fill the gaps of the brief picture of myself which I have presented here. Please feel free to ask any questions about me, I will be more than glad to answer them. In asking your permission for your daughter's hand in marriage I wish to assure you that I fully realize the responsibilities of a husband.

We will set our wedding date upon your approval and acknowledgment of this letter. Since we have never met, I can only ask your acceptance of me on the basis of faith. Please feel free to offer any suggestions. Thank you.

My sincere regards and best wishes to both of you, and I hope to hear from you soon.

Very sincerely yours, Edward Lumsdaine

Our daughter Anne has archived all of the letters her mother had written to her parents in Switzerland, and she made a file of those covering key events for her brothers.

The summer passed in a whirlwind. We looked for a small apartment to rent and found a garage that had been converted into a furnished place behind a house on Ocean Avenue. It was affordable with its minimal kitchen, a small metal table with two chairs, an old sofa, a small desk, a dresser, a small wardrobe, and a double bed. The bed promptly collapsed when we sat on it, which caused us to break out in a gale of laughter. The apartment had a cement floor, and we discovered later it also had termites.

In mid-August, Monika moved in and sewed her own wedding dress with a machine borrowed from friends. Regrettably, we never did get to go flying together—it would have been a unique memory. But we had to use our meager resources to set up housekeeping and take care of other financial commitments, like paying for my auto accident and supporting my mother.

The evening before our wedding, I stopped by before going to work to ask Monika if my lacy pocket-handkerchief was ready. We were both stressed out—she was putting the finishing touches on her wedding dress—but I was startled at her indignant response. She later told me, that she had been afraid her response would cause me to call off the wedding.

Monika's Comments

In February 1959, for my birthday, Esther Langford gave me a surprise birthday party. She invited a dozen girls from college—I can't imagine how she found out who were my closest friends. Never before had I heard of such a thing as a surprise party. It was wonderful, and the girls pooled their gift together—an envelope with enough money for a couple of hours of flying. During the days after Edward had first kissed me, I must have sat around the Langford's home all dreamy-eyed. Esther commented that she felt sorry for my mother who missed this special time when her daughter seriously fell in love.

By mid-summer, with school expenses and the wedding coming up, there was no more money for further flying. I did pass the written exam for the commercial pilot's license, with a score of 70%. Even though I was never to pilot another plane, I still remember the incredible view of the golden foothills around Ventura and the blue Pacific with the Channel Islands. Years later, when my sister Lili got a pilot's license, she was disappointed I never went flying with her or took up the offer of a flight in a glider by one of her pilot friends.

I have beautiful memories of two trips during the spring of 1959, before I fell in love with Edward. One was a trip to San Francisco with the Langfords. Artie could take two friends along, and we girls shared a room at the TraveLodge. The highlight was walking about halfway across the Golden Gate Bridge. I also very much enjoyed learning more about the chain of missions established by Spanish Franciscan priests between 1769 and 1823. They were the ones who introduced vineyards and orange groves to California. On this trip, we visited the restored mission of San Gabriel in Carmel with its gorgeous garden. I never dreamed I would be married in one of these mission churches.

The second trip was with Ray and Peggy York, who took me to Death Valley, followed by Kings Canyon and Sequoia National Parks in the Sierra Nevada. The photo shows Peggy with me in a covered wagon. We slept in sleeping bags in the open, and I was utterly amazed at the night sky in Death Valley; it felt as if I were about to fall into the immensity of space and the Milky Way with its myriad stars. Death Valley is known for being the lowest point in the US. This contrasted a few days later with the experience of camping along a rushing stream among the giant redwood trees—another incredible sight. I learned more about pioneers and visited ghost towns; this was different than learning about this part of American history from books.

During that spring, I saw a movie with Ingrid Bergman, *The Inn of the Sixth Happiness*. I loved the story based on the life of missionary to China, Gladys Aylward, but I have no recollection who invited me to the cinema. Edward took me on a date to a drive-in theatre to see *House on Haunted Hill*. This was a new experience for me, and I sat entranced during the entire show, paying scant attention to him. He was disappointed I did not turn to him for comfort during scary scenes.

Edward and I loved to sunbathe at Ventura beach on weekends, even though by early summer the water was still too cold for swimming. This was the first technicolor slide of my sweetheart I sent to my parents.

After Edward returned from his training in the Air Force Reserve at Madera, I came down with a rash all over my face and body. I went to see a German doctor, who attributed this outbreak to stress. No wonder—I had a difficult decision to make, choosing one of three hard options:

1. *Return to Switzerland:* My father had proposed that I could continue to study construction drawing at the newly opened Technical School in Lucerne, and I had already checked out my flight reservation with a travel agent in Ojai in early August. Edward and I would continue our courtship by mail until he could come to Switzerland for the wedding in a year or so.
2. *Continuing my studies at Ventura College* while staying with Ralph and Natalie Sylvester who had offered to sponsor me. He was our mechanical drawing instructor. This would enable me to earn an Associate of Arts degree and would give me time to get to know Edward better during a longer engagement period.
3. *Getting married as soon as legally possible,* which would be September 8.

We didn't discuss Option 2 much. I didn't want to be dependent on another American family for my support since I had no way of earning my keep under the terms of a student visa. Also, we were very much attracted to each other, and it would have been difficult to practice restraint for a year with a lot of unchaperoned time together.

Both my parents and Edward urged me to take Option 1. One thought scared me about returning to Switzerland—out of sight, out of mind. I just knew I had found the perfect mate for me, and I didn't want to be separated from him and take the risk that he might not wait for me, perhaps falling in love with someone else. To tell the truth, in the back of my mind I did not want to leave America, a country in which I felt more at home than in my native Switzerland. Edward only recently confessed that he saw this decision as a test of my commitment to him. Had I left, his feelings of rejection would have kept him from writing to me, thus ending our relationship. Am I ever glad I did not choose Option 1—returning to Switzerland.

This left Option 3—to marry quickly. Was this the best choice? Would I have chosen differently if I had been more mature? By rushing into marriage, we created difficulties for ourselves that took a long time to surmount. However, I have come to believe God made us for each other. In later days when asked, we counseled other young couples to take the time for getting to know one another on a deeper level before marriage, but in our unique circumstances, this was not realistic.

As far as I was concerned, I was overwhelmed that I had gained a smart and handsome fellow who professed to love me, having never been in a serious relationship with anyone before. In those days, most guys were not interested in a woman who might be more intelligent than they were.

More importantly, I sensed that Edward needed me, having felt rejected by his own family as a child and teenager. Neither of us was well prepared for marriage or had good role models of a true partnership of equals in our parents. Neither did we have supportive, experienced, close friends our age with whom we could share our qualms and concerns. Both of us kept our emotions under lock and key—so it is doubtful if we would have been willing to listen to advice from any source. For better or for worse, we felt we only had each other to lean on. In our eyes, this was enough.

CHAPTER EIGHT

Edward: With This Ring

This is a facsimile of the letter I received from my future father-in-law, including his letterhead.

Angelo Amsler, Ingenieur
Gottfried Keller Strasse 10
Kriens
Telefon (041) 3 05 92

6th August, 1959.

Dear Mr. Lumsdaine,

We have received your letter of 16th July, of which we come to know, that you feel sorry to be engaged to Monika without having asked us in advance for our permission. How could we be cross with you, as even our own daughter has not asked us for permission to be engaged to you. By the time I got engaged I also did not ask my wife's mother for permission. Asking the parents is usual where one lives close together and knows each other personally.

It seems to us unintelligible that you like to marry so quickly, as you are both so young. One is not used to that here in Europe. And as Monika already told us that she wishes to have a baby at once I begged to require for information about your conditions in income and the living expenses in Ventura, before I should come to an understanding for the marriage. As Monika has described the circumstances to us, it would be possible for you, in fact of the GI-Bill, to make sufficient savings, in order to buy a housing-establishment before long. With that, we have annulled our vetoes to the marriage and wish Monika good luck and blessings. Herewith we have also given you our agreement for marriage to our daughter. We welcome you therefore formally as member of our family and hope to make your personal acquaintance very soon. We feel free to call you Edward now.

It almost seems as if we see the marriage only from the material side. But this is not true in any way.

Certainly, certain material foundations are indispensable, but important is the existence of true love and affection which appears to be the real reason for marriage. Monika is an intellectual, well-educated and characterful young person and therefore I well may trust that she found in you just the same partner for life. In this regard we put faith in you, like Monika does, who knows you of course better than we do. Help our daughter to everlasting happiness, it will also be yours. Our agreement to the marriage requires that Monika keeps her Swiss citizenship; this could be very important in certain circumstances. I think Monika already spoke about this matter.

We hope that the future will show that we can speak proudly about you and send you our best wishes for the new part of life.

Yours sincerely,

A. Amsler *R. Amsler*

Best of luck and good wishes, Lili

A day or two after I received this letter, I thoughtfully wrote to Monika's father on blue airmail stationary which folded to form an envelope (he marked it as #51):

Dear Mr. and Mrs. Amsler, *16th August 1959*

Thank you very much for your letter of 6th August; I was very anxious and glad to receive it. Summer school ended on the 14th of August and the Fall Semester won't begin until September the 14th. This gives Monika and me ample time to make the necessary preparations for our wedding.

We have set the wedding date for the 8th of September (the day after Labor Day) in order to have almost a week for our honeymoon before school begins. We have planned to spend this week in San Francisco. I have also advised Monika to remain a Swiss citizen and she agrees readily. I am very glad because Switzerland is a country she can always be proud of.

We do not plan to remain here in the United States after my graduation from College; my plans are to obtain a job from a firm which has offices in Europe. This shouldn't be hard to do, because most Americans prefer to work here at home. I think Monika has explained to you my plans for completing college.

(First flap): *A man working full time and attending College is perhaps rather unusual in Europe, and I must confess that it is also unheard of in Shanghai, but it is very common here. For example at Ventura College, approximately 30-50 percent of students work part time, 20% work full time, and the rest have the support of their parents.*

(Second flap): *I am convinced that Monika and I will be very happy together, and although life is never without hardships and disappointments, I am sure we will be able to see it through together.*

With very best wishes and sincere regards to you both and to Miss Amsler,

Yours, Edward Lumsdaine

I insisted that we marry in the Catholic church. Although Monika was Protestant in her beliefs, she agreed. Half her relatives and most of her schoolmates in Switzerland were Catholic, and thus this faith was familiar to her. Since my siblings were Catholic, I did not want them to think I was being controlled by my wife by not marrying in a Catholic church. Besides, I still felt close to the Jesuit Brothers from school in Shanghai, and I also wanted to honor Father Des and Father Peter who had helped me—I felt obligated to be faithful to the Catholic religion. In addition, at that time, attending a church of a different denomination was considered to be a sin.

Miss Monika Edith Amsler
and
Mr. Edward Lumsdaine
announce their marriage
on Tuesday, the eighth of September
nineteen hundred and fifty-nine
Ventura, California

Six days before our wedding, we picked up 75 simple announcements from the printer for $10.92, for handing out or mailing to close relatives, friends, and colleagues.

We wanted to be married in the historic Mission Church of San Buenaventura. We had premarital meetings with Father O'Reilly and had to sign papers that our children would be baptized and raised Catholic before he agreed to marry us in his church. Subsequently, we would attend mass there almost every Sunday until we moved away from Ventura.

I worked the graveyard shift the day of our wedding, which was a Tuesday, with Monday having been Labor Day that year. Then I asked to have the rest of the week off to take Monika on a brief honeymoon trip. I tried to snatch a nap around 8:30 am, but was too nervous to fall asleep. The wedding was set for 2 pm, and the Yorks treated us to a special lunch at the swanky Pierpont Inn. On my way back to Chuck's place after the meal to get dressed for the wedding, I had a minor fender bender. A car suddenly pulled out of a driveway in front of me and I could not avoid a collision. This mishap made me late to church. Monika was on pins and needles until I appeared abou ten minutes late.

Chuck was my best man, and George, Maria and Bob represented the rest of my family. Milly did not attend the ceremony, as she was babysitting Maria and Bob's three children. My friends Chris and Bill were joined by several of Monika's college friends, as well as the Langfords, Yorks, Sylvesters, and Muenzers. Irwin Muenzer was Austrian, and Elsie was Swiss. They were neighbors of the Yorks—that's how Monika got to know them.

When Father O'Reilly asked, "Do you, John, take this woman, Monika, to be your lawful wedded wife?" Ray York came close to stopping the wedding. He thought I was getting married under an assumed name. He was relieved when I explained the Catholic Church had used my baptism name for the ceremony. The marriage service lasted only about fifteen minutes, and we paused quickly outside in the garden to have a photo taken with Father O'Reilly. Monika later wrote to her parents that I had given her only a tiny kiss at the altar after our vows were spoken. She was very surprised at being showered with rice as we exited the church. This wedding custom was new to her.

Afterwards, Ray and Peggy York kindly hosted a small reception in their home on the hill for us, and they lent us a large "Just Married" placard from their own wedding the year before. Chris and Bill tied the traditional old shoes and beer cans to the bumper of a used blue '53 Ford I had bought recently. For our honeymoon trip, Monika changed into a blue summer dress she had sewn herself, as seen in the photo with Bob, Maria, Chuck and George.

The wedding cost me only $25 for Monika's flowers and a contribution to the church, plus a small fee for the mandatory blood tests and the marriage license. Peggy had generously bought flowers for the church.

We still have the receipt for the two wedding rings bought on 31 August 1959 at Alberts Jewelers for a total of $64.26. Our wedding rings were made with a base of yellow gold, topped with a narrower band of white gold sculpted in a faceted zig-zag pattern. Monika lost hers some ten years later in South Dakota while raking fall leaves. We replaced it, and it was on her finger for 48 years. But during a spell of hot weather, her finger swelled up and became so painful, that she had to get a jeweler to cut off the ring. She had it refashioned into a pendant on a gold chain that had belonged to her sister, combined with a blue topaz that I bought for her in Rio de Janeiro. I can't remember when I lost my ring. I did not replace it because it was uncomfortable.

We almost lost our lives on the drive to San Francisco. We left around 4 o'clock in the afternoon after the wedding reception. By then I had been up for close to twenty-four hours. We were on a two-lane stretch of highway past Santa Barbara when I fell asleep at the wheel. My new wife had also dozed off. Incredibly, I felt a tap on my shoulder to wake up just in time to avoid a head-on crash with an oncoming car. After this, I asked Monika to keep me awake for the rest of the way by talking to me.

Two hours later, we noticed a pickup truck was following us very closely. When I slowed down, it slowed down; when I accelerated, it accelerated. Even when we passed other cars or let other cars and trucks pass us, we could not shake it. It was rather uncanny since most of these stretches of the two-lane highway were very dark. Only when we pulled into a gas station near Gilroy, we finally were rid of this unwelcome "shadow." Now thinking back on this, we're wondering if it was yet another providential occurrence to keep us alert.

We were very tired and glad to find the small Marina Motel on Lombard Street near the Golden Gate. We picked up a bottle of champagne in a store across the street, then were too tired to celebrate but immediately went to sleep. We savored it the next morning with some left-over wedding cake that Peggy had packed up for us. It seems incredible that the cost for this AAA-recommended lodging was only $8.50, to be paid in advance.

I enjoyed showing off to my bride that I knew my way around San Francisco. She especially liked the Golden Gate Bridge, the drive around the Bay, and riding the cable cars. We made a brief stop at Horace's so I could introduce my wife to him. That was the last time I saw Horace. A few years ago, my sister Maria happened to read the obituaries in the *San Francisco Chronicle* and noticed he was over ninety-two when he died.

Monika's Comments

At the reception in Peggy and Ray's home, we found a small table with cards and wedding gifts. All the gifts were practical, ranging from towels and bedsheets to dishes, tablemats and other kitchenware, such as mixing bowls

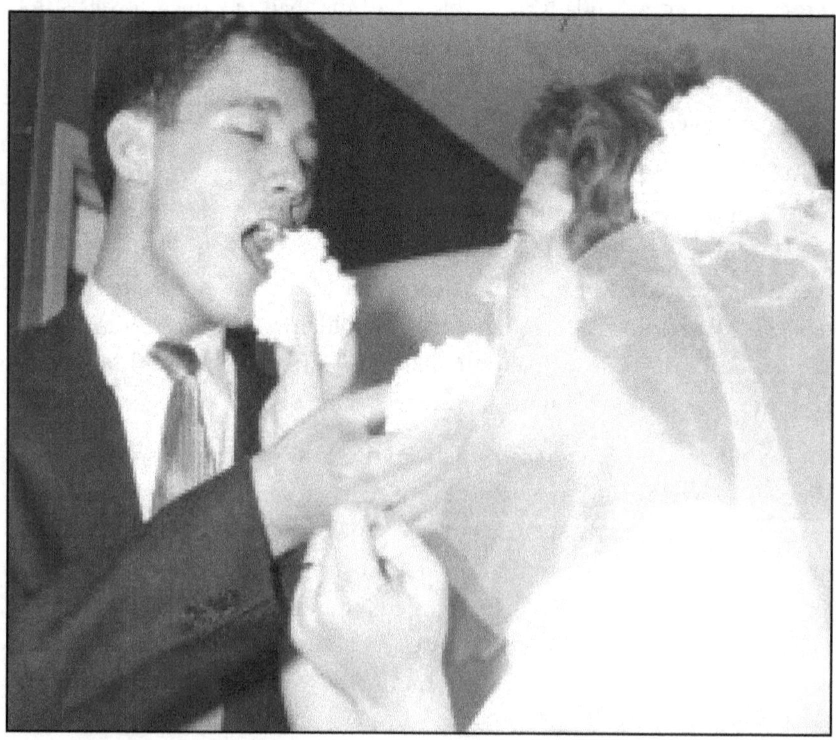

and a toaster. We were touched by the blue china set from the Sylvesters—it had belonged to Natalie's grandmother. The gift that lasted the longest, about 30 years, was a Presto electric skillet from the Yorks. There was a generous check from the Langfords that helped pay for our honeymoon expenses. I also appreciated a wooden ironing board with a steam iron from the Muenzers.

I was glad when the old shoes and cans dropped off our car a few miles into our drive toward San Francisco, but sorry that the "Just Married" sign also disappeared somewhere along the way—we had planned to return it to Peggy and Ray.

I felt greatly relieved we actually were married in church! I did not care then that it was just a very simple ceremony. Now, so many years later, I have some regrets that I did not think more of myself to realize it would be important to have our wedding be a real family celebration and to give Edward's father and my parents enough notice to be able to attend.

Here are the congratulations we received from my family on our marriage.

Herzliche Glückwünsche zur Vermählung

Dear Monika: Mameli bought this pretty card for your wedding day. We wish you, dear child, a beautiful, happy day. No, our wishes go much farther, we wish you a happy life at the side of a dear, admirable spouse by name of Edward.

Dear Edward: We welcome you as our son, and ask you to call us from now on Mami and Papi. Our heartfelt wishes may accompany you all the days of your life.

We all send you both our best wishes for a happy life together, and may it bring you many blessings!

With all our love, Papi, Mami and Lili

Excerpts of some letters in the next chapter show our attempts at navigating family relationships beyond the small circle centered on just the two of us.

CHAPTER NINE

Edward: Starting Married Life in a Garage

Although part of my allotment from the GI Bill was still going to my mother, my portion increased because of marriage. With this and with full-time work, we were doing well financially, especially by living in the low-rent, tiny converted garage apartment. The photo shows the kitchen corner. It didn't take much to set up housekeeping, and we appreciated the practical wedding gifts we had received. Eventually, Monika's father had her books and adult belongings (except winter clothes) shipped to her in a custom-made crate. She was especially glad to finally have her silverware given to her by her godparents over several years. Also included was an Elna sewing machine—her parents' wedding gift.

In the meantime, Monika quickly learned to eat with chopsticks. When I came home from work after midnight, we enjoyed a snack of fruit, cheese and homemade bread, while listening to semi-classical music on the radio. We had bought the radio to listen to the Nixon-Kennedy debates. I found our setup cozy and comfortable, but I think it was quite a letdown for Monika from her middle-class upbringing. She also did not like that I continued smoking, especially in bed, although she didn't complain much.

I did not want Monika to work—I felt very protective of her and wanted to provide for all our needs. Thus, she stayed home, knitting, learning to cook, and helping me with my homework. She was an excellent tutor. I did not have time to read the assigned Greek tragedies in my literature course. Monika, on the other hand, had always been a voracious reader. She read my book assignments, summarized the material, and before an exam briefed me on all the important points. I could ask her questions, and she quizzed me on my understanding of the material. I was learning more from her interesting discussions than from the instructor's lectures. He was one of the sports coaches, not trained as an English teacher. This was great for me because it enabled me to pass the exams with A's or B's, and I felt I was bonding with Monika more deeply. I was speechless when decades later, an educator commented that this was cheating, instead of appreciating that I had a superior learning environment with my private tutor.

Also, Monika enjoyed neatly transcribing my scribbled math homework and carefully plotted complicated graphs. I still have these spiral-bound notebooks! She used to tease me sometimes, saying, "You only married me because you needed help with drawing." It's a good thing this was not true—once computers came with CAD software and math graphics, she was out of *that* job.

Here is a letter in green ink on pale green stationary. Monika wrote it to me for my birthday three weeks after we were married. It is a good reminder to us of what we had during our honeymoon period, and what I almost lost years later when I took her for granted and had other priorities in my life.

My Dear Beloved Husband,

For your birthday I wish you the very, very best! I want to make this new year of your life the happiest you ever had. You are such an adorable man, such a sweet husband, and such a considerate and wonderful lover – I wish I really could tell it to you in words how deeply I love you, how much affection, and admiration, and passion I have for you in my heart. You are the center, and the joy, the light and the meaning of my life, and I hope so much that I always can be near you and take care of you and make your life wonderful, too.

You are so lovable, so infinitely sweet to me. I love you, I love the way you think and feel, I love the expression on your face, your dear face, when you tell me that you love me, I love all the ways you show me your love for me, I love your laughing, your jokes, your voice, your smiles; I even love you when you are tired, or grumpy, or angry at me. I love to just look at you and marvel that you, you wonderful you, are really all mine, and only mine, and I still can hardly believe it. I love to wait for your coming home at night. I love your contentment when I rub your back. I love just everything about you. I love when, sometimes, you look like a little boy, and when, sometimes, you are so much more experienced, and realistic, and clever and sensible and older than me. I am so proud to be your wife!

I have complete faith in you. To me you are a tower of strength, and when I am sad about something, or worried, I always have your understanding and consolation. I need you so much, my Sweetheart.

So fortunate I am to have you and to belong to you! With you, everything is bearable and wonderful! Life is just simply wonderful with you!

Happy Birthday! With love, Your Wife

Chuck, Maria, George, and I were all saving money to pay for the rest of the family to come to the US. There were many forms to sign and get notarized before all the paperwork for my mother's visa was complete and the family was finally reunited in America in April 1960. Monika and I barely remember being asked to drive to San Francisco to pick up Robert and Philip. After living near Maria in Long Beach for a while, my parents moved to Ventura, where my father found a job as a janitor in a laundromat. Philip and Robert began attending Ventura College and found work around the area. One of the jobs was picking apples at the Langfords, and there was a stint as waiters at the Ojai Valley Inn. However, with all of us working and studying, we rarely saw them for fun or even just for a simple meal.

I soon traded in the old Ford for a used black VW Beetle with a pretty blue and white interior and flippers instead of turn signals. It was a stick shift, and I tried to teach Monika how to drive it. After she ground the gears a few times, I couldn't bear it and stopped the lessons. One good outcome from her taking the exam for a learner's permit showed that she needed eyeglasses.

Monika got bored with taking care of our tiny place—there was really nothing much for her to do. I suggested she go back to college, at least part-time. I was pleased she chose to major in mathematics. We both took classes during the summer and fall of 1960. We both got A's in calculus from the same instructor, even though she took the course a semester after I did. I was proud of her.

Once, when Monika did a physics experiment, the recording strip caught on fire. I happened to be in the classroom next door, heard a startled exclamation, recognized her voice, and rushed to the rescue. It took but a few seconds to tear the strip off, stomp on it with my big shoes, and extinguish the flames. The instructor was not in the room at the time.

I felt good about being married, and I tried to ignore one little problem. I became jealous whenever Monika even glanced at other guys. I tended to forget that this country was still new to her; she was interested in people and curious about Americans and their customs and ways of talking. Nevertheless, I saw the "*mahjong* piece of marriage" had fallen into place neatly.

I no longer doubted I could make it in engineering. I was accepted and treated with respect by my instructors and fellow students at school, as well as by my peers and supervisors at work. With this increase in self-confidence, I decided it was time for us to move on to a *real* university.

Monika's Comments

As a newly married housewife, I had a lot to learn. The only thing I knew to cook well was spaghetti. I even managed to burn soup—although that was the fault of the old pot we found on a trash pile. Our neighbors gave us some squabs; it took me a whole day to pluck them and cook them, resulting in only a few tasty morsels since they were very tiny birds. I baked bread from a Swiss recipe. This bread was crusty and delicious at first, but turned stone-hard the next day. It took me a while to realize I needed to add more liquids to Swiss recipes: apparently, flour in the US was drier than in Switzerland. For a break away from the apartment, Edward would drive us to Santa Barbara or Ojai, or he took me to dinner at El Tecolote, an inexpensive but authentic Mexican restaurant near Camarillo.

I was surprised when a tall man knocked at the door one evening while Edward was at work and said: "I am Eddie's Uncle Art." My husband had neglected to mention that he had this uncle. After some probing questions, I was finally convinced and served him a snack of buttered bread and fruit.

Since I had vehemently vowed to my classmates in high school that I would never marry, it was a big surprise when I turned out to be the first one of our class to do so. With both of us coming from different cultures and learning to adjust to life in America as a young married couple, it is no wonder that we encountered problems and had many misunderstandings, some stemming from the fact that English was not our mother tongue. For example, when I used the word "screw" in its meaning of a fastener, Edward took it as the vulgar term and told me not to talk like that. We did not realize for many years that good communication is crucial to a good marriage. We are still learning.

It wasn't just getting adjusted to one person—there was an entire extended family I had to get to know. I had of course met Ed's brothers. Chuck and George, in Ventura and Maria and her husband, Bob, on a weekend visit to Long Beach. Over the next year, I would meet not just Uncle Art, but his mother (by letter), and then Dad, Mom, Robert, Philip, Albert, Milly and Dolly when they were reunited with the family in California. Our marriage created quite a stir, as attested by the following letters.

The first one was from Edward's father, typed and dated Saturday, Dec. 5, 1959:

Dear Ed & Monika:
Received your letter of November 29, as well as the photos. Really Ed, you looked happier at the prospect of eating, than in the one which I presume was taken immediately after the ceremony.

Well, come end of last September, Ed, you were 22 years old, and that certainly is not too early to get married. I also received a letter from Maria, indicating that they had visited you for Thanksgiving. Conversations with a Mr. Chang of American President Lines has led to a possibility of Mom and the rest of the children coming to the United States by a vessel from Hong Kong either on April 25 or May 25, 1960. According to Maria, this is contingent upon a deposit of $500 by January of next year.

So yesterday, I mailed my check for $500 to the American President Lines (even though I have just lost my job). On top of that I received a letter from Philip in Hong Kong, asking me to send Mom $100 so they could clean things up and make a better impression before leaving. Apparently, they are anxious to leave as soon as it can be arranged. Maria mentioned about your putting up $300 eventually for Mom and the kids.

With much love to both of you, Dad

Then here is a letter from Edward's step-grandmother from Seattle, dated Sunday, 13 December 1959. It was handwritten with red ballpoint pen, and I have treasured it for all these years. Sadly, I never had a chance to meet her, as she died in 1962. She is buried in Seattle where we saw her grave a few years ago when we attended her grandson David's funeral. From what we have heard from her son Art, she had an unusually loving and forgiving heart.

Dear Ed,

I was very happy to receive your letter and Monika's. I knew of your marriage because Maria was a good girl and had written me about it. No hurt feelings, I assure you, but just wanted to hear from you and it was very sweet of Monika to also write.

I wasn't too greatly surprised because I had already been thinking that both you and Charlie had reached the age when either of you might meet the one right girl. – I do hope you will be very happy and from Maria's letter and Art's report, and my own "long distance" opinion, I believe you have every chance for a good marriage, and I feel happy for you..

Art wrote me as soon as he had seen you and I was very glad he could meet Monika—and alone—that way he could become better acquainted with her in a short time. I value his judgment of people and he was much pleased that you have married a girl like Monika.

All my very best wishes for your happiness and success. I hear from your father every week or two and he writes you are all still working toward bringing your mother and the other children to the US. Don't give up, one day your efforts will be successful and Philip can have the advantages you are so eager for him to acquire. Do write occasionally when you have time, and all of you have a very Happy Christmas.

With much love, Grandmother

Dear Monika,

Thank you so much for your sweet letter. I do greatly appreciate your writing and trust you will continue to do it, so we shall become better acquainted. You are a long way from your own family, so if you at any time feel pangs of homesickness and need to unburden your feelings to someone who is a mother and knows what separation means to all of us at times, please feel free to write me. Many of Art's friends have done just that many times. Art enjoyed so much his brief visit with you and I'm so glad he saw you. Art is very fond of his nephews and nieces. I love having the pictures, and thank you both for them. All the very best wishes in the world for your happiness.

With much love, Grandmother.

P.S. If you don't feel like calling me "Grandmother" you can just call me "Gerry." All Art's children (my grandchildren) call me "Gerry" and so do Art and Marion and all Art's friends.

I was very thankful for Gerry's letter, and I did pour out my heart to her once when one of my new in-laws had said some unkind words about me marrying Edward "just for a meal ticket."

On Christmas morning in 1960, we drove to Lake Matilija near Ojai to just have a relaxing time together. We talked about having many children, and Edward shared some more of his feelings about the hard times he endured in Shanghai. I again was so glad we had married—he needed me to love him and appreciate him, and I was still in awe that someone special like him actually wanted *me*.

Afterwards, we went to Mom and Dad's house for the rest of Christmas Day. I was often uncomfortable in the family because everyone spoke Chinese, and it sounded to me like they were arguing, sometimes vehemently. Edward did not do a lot of translating for me, so I felt rather out of place. On the other hand, I started to enjoy eating the Chinese food that my mother-in-law cooked, although it took a while until I really got to like *lap chong*, the sausage. Over time, she taught me how to make *bao* and spring rolls. Both are very time-consuming to prepare, and I haven't often had the time or energy for this task.

This photo was taken in the plain backyard of the garage apartment. The only nice surprise were pink amaryllis blooms that popped up in the fall of 1960 along the stoop. The black and white dress was a gift from Edward's sister Maria. I was pleased that it fit me so well.

But by this time, Edward had made a decision that would soon take us a long distance from his family, as he describes in the next four chapters. Both of us were looking forward to this new adventure in the Southwest!

Years later, while visiting family in the Los Angeles area, we started on a drive to Ventura to visit the college and see if our first little apartment was still there. We soon noticed huge black clouds of smoke and heard warnings on the radio to avoid the roads to Ventura because of a large wildfire. We turned around so as not to miss our flight home. Edward was to visit the college decades later, but I never saw it again.

CHAPTER TEN

Edward: Moving to the Desert

I was still intrigued by the wonder of flying, and thus aeronautical engineering grew to be my career goal. However, in the late fifties and early sixties, very few universities that I could get into or afford offered programs in aeronautics. Thus, I fixed on the related but more marketable degree of mechanical engineering. The next task was to choose where I wanted to continue my education. My grades in Ventura College had steadily improved since my marriage to Monika. I could now get into the University of California at Berkeley. Although the tuition was reasonable, we did not have enough income to cover the living expenses there.

We learned from our counselor that, given our financial situation, the best bet was to transfer to New Mexico State University in Las Cruces. An efficiency apartment in married student housing would cost only $30 per month, utilities included. We had enough money saved to pay one year of out-of-state tuition for both of us until we were eligible to become residents of New Mexico and would qualify for the much lower in-state tuition. This turned out to be a good gamble financially—we successively moved up to a one-bedroom apartment, a two-bedroom apartment, and then a small single-family house at $59 per month with a private backyard that included a clothes line and a lawn. Monika could easily continue her studies, since she was majoring in mathematics.

There was one major problem with moving to New Mexico. In the mid-1950s I had lived in racially segregated Mississippi. Interracial marriage did not become legal in the South until 1967. Although Las Cruces was in the Southwest, the word "South" put a lot of discomfort in my heart. After I was officially admitted, I wrote to the Admissions Office, explaining my apprehensions about going to school in the Southwest and asking if there was any racial discrimination. In response, I received a glowing report about Las Cruces being a tri-cultural and tolerant area. So, under the mandatory race category on the pre-registration form, I confidently entered "Caucasian." I felt I had as much a right to be Caucasian as Asian. Without another thought I mailed off the form.

For the move Monika and I stuffed all our belongings up to the ceiling into our little VW Beetle, except for one box of books shipped parcel-post at the special low rate of five cents a pound. We had to abandon the little bookshelf we had built from cement blocks and the boards from my father's shipping crate, because it had become infested with termites.

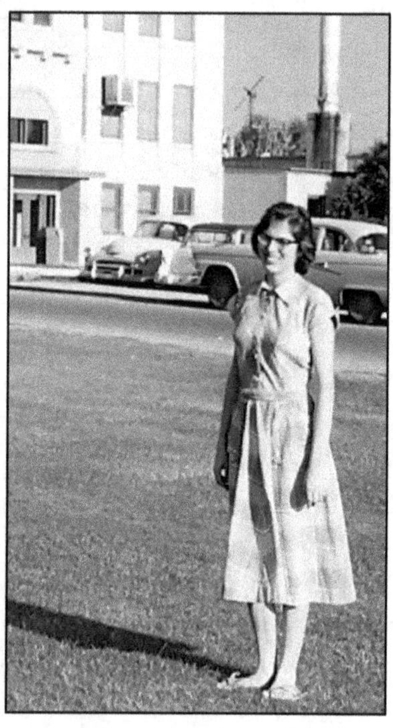

The photos on campus show me on the lawn fronting the Administration Building and Monika standing near the oldest engineering building soon after we arrived at NMSU in January 1961.

The first day I reported for school, the registrar, Ira Renfro, took one look at me, scratched out "Caucasian" on the registration form, and replaced it with "Chinese," ostensibly because I looked oriental and my birthplace was Hong Kong. I protested to the administration in writing, but she denied my request to reverse the change. In a face-to-face meeting she told me, "You have no right to claim to be white when you have colored blood mixed in you and look Chinese." But having the transcript say "Caucasian" was important for economic reasons. Everything being equal, a Caucasian had an advantage in landing a job or at least an interview. By 1972, my transcript still showed "Chinese." Today, I am sure I could have this entry deleted.

I was surprised it took me a while to get acclimated to the altitude of Las Cruces, having lived at sea level all my life. The contrast between flowering Ventura in winter and the stark desert was quite a shock. Eventually, the wide sky and open desert landscape grew on us, and we came to feel we were suffocating when we traveled to areas with many trees. Monika especially enjoyed the view of the Organ Mountains to the east.

We learned a new culture where rodeos were weekly events and where Billy the Kid, Geronimo, and Pancho Villa were local heroes. We loved to drive out to White Sands National Monument one hour away to climb the unique gypsum dunes. Less pleasant were the occasional sand storms. Our barrack housing had many cracks, and soon there would be a layer of thick dust across our papers when studying and grit between our teeth when eating.

I immediately received junior standing at New Mexico State University with complete transfer credit for all required freshman and sophomore courses. Monika and I enjoyed being *real* college students now that I was able to devote myself to full-time study without having to work. We also began to attend football games and other sports events, plays, and concerts.

But I couldn't shake my chronic tiredness. When I developed a low-grade fever, I finally went to see a doctor. Two letters describe this first health crisis since our marriage. The first letter was written by Monika, (identified as #112 by her father and dated 11 April 1961). I wrote the second letter (#113 and dated 17 April 1961) with a postscript by Monika.

Lieber Papi,
Thank you for your letter, and we are very thankful for sending the check with the remainder of my savings account in Switzerland, which came at an opportune time, as our cupboards were getting bare. Your letter made a detour; it was stamped in Mexico three days ago. The Veterans Administration is again in a mess, and it will be weeks before we will get the stipend from the GI Bill. They seem to be confused that the semester in Ventura ended on Feb 2 and the semester here started on Jan 31. They only pay for the days Edward is in school, and he couldn't have been in two places at the same time. He's had to write several letters already, trying to explain that he left Ventura right after the last final exam, not on the last official semester end which was a few days later.

Edward for the first time had no fever today, and in a day or two he can return to classes, as allowed by the doctor. He's had to take four pills every day, and each one cost 50 cents. To celebrate his recovery, I cooked sweet-and-sour pork today, with fresh green asparagus, rice, and a lettuce/ tomato salad. I'm glad we were able to buy fresh fruit today: grapefruit, oranges, apples, bananas and a melon.

Thanks again for everything, Monika and Edward

Dear Papi, Mameli, and Lili,

It is really unfortunate that I should fall ill and that it took the doctors such a long time (1 month) to diagnose my illness. After being treated for various types of infections I was finally admitted to the hospital on Thursday, 13 April 1961, for observation and tests. On Friday afternoon the doctor told me that I have hepatitis A (virus infection of the liver, likely caught from contaminated food or water). I was released from the hospital Saturday. Treatment consists of a high protein diet and complete bed rest. It feels rather awkward to eat, wash, do my homework, and write letters in bed. Monika is very patient and takes very good care of me. She is a wonderful wife!!! The school insurance paid for the hospital bill but did not pay for doctor visits or the medicine. I should be able to finish this semester since my condition only requires physical but not mental rest. I can get up in time to take final exams.

Best wishes and love, Edward

P.S. Lieber Papi, liebes Mameli: Since Edward's letter, he got sick again, worse than before. When his eyes turned all yellow, I called another doctor, the best in the city, and when he saw Edward, he said he had to immediately go into the hospital. It was easy for me to visit him, since the bus stops right in front of our apartment building. Then I moved the furniture around, so Edward would have more fresh air by being close to the windows. I'm pretty busy with my homework and bringing Edward's homework to his teachers. Because he has never been sick before, this is very difficult for him.

I got an injection of gamma globulin into the hip, as a precautionary measure. For two days, I could hardly sit down. Otherwise, the weather here is hot as usual. Yesterday I cooked liver with a lot of onions. I used a bit of vinegar, since I did not have any wine. Mameli, please send me your recipe.

A thousand kisses to you all, Monika

The high-protein diet consisted mainly of a lot of cottage cheese—I got quite sick of it by the end of this treatment. All my instructors agreed to my continuing in their classes if I could keep up with homework and come in to take exams. Every day, Monika made the rounds to turn in my problem sets and pick up new assignments. My thermodynamics instructor was not happy when I made the highest grade in the final exam without having attended his lectures. I finished the term with all A's and B's except for a two-credit C in instrumentation, the only C grade I ever earned at NMSU.

Each term I took an extra load of classes with the Vice-President's permission. Just being admitted and going to a university was a big achievement for me, and I have always been thankful for the opportunity. Had I remained in China or lived almost anywhere else in the world at that time, there would not have been any second chance to get a higher education. What amazed me most about the US was that I could have as many chances as I needed, and I found over time that a number of different paths were opening to me. I thought it was the height of stupidity, that some kids whose parents offered to pay for their college education would not take advantage of it.

We lived in barracks left over from World War II. Each one was subdivided into five to seven apartments with little soundproofing in between. Occasionally, we would get together as couples to play games, but mostly everyone was busy studying or working. Every two weeks the barracks were fumigated. Following each treatment, we swept up a dustpan full of dead cockroaches.

There was a small fenced front yard, and Monika planted a few flowers along the edge of the walkway. The back yard between the barracks had a clothesline for each apartment, and we also appreciated the shade trees.

Although Monika and I got along well when studying, we had a hard time adjusting to our differences. I had few earthly possessions and was not accustomed to planning for the future. Based on my experiences while growing up, I felt it was too unpredictable. However, Monika was not brought up that way. She began to worry and tried to plan for every conceivable contingency. I was in the habit of clamming up when something bothered me. On occasion I would not talk to her for two weeks beyond the bare essentials without letting her know the cause of my emotional withdrawal.

Once, I abruptly and wordlessly left our apartment while she was doing dishes and something snapped. She came to the door as I was walking toward the garden gate on a concrete path. When I would not stop or respond to her, she threw the orange coffee cup she happened to hold in her hand. It shattered on the path, and one large shard cut deeply into my calf. This incident scared both of us—I stopped giving her the silent treatment, and she never threw anything at me again. However, the habit of hiding my hurts continued for a long time. Only recently have I been able to start talking about my feelings.

On Friday, October 13, 1961, *The Ventura (California) County Star-Free Press* published the following article about us.

INTERNATIONAL COUPLE AT COLLEGE

Edward Lumsdaines Earn Honors

Mr. and Mrs. Edward Lumsdaine of Ventura are an unusual married student couple at New Mexico State University.

Although neither is a native-born American and might be expected to encounter language difficulties, both earned academic honors during the spring semester at NMSU.

They earned the honors while majoring in two of the toughest study programs at the university—mathematics and engineering. To make it more difficult, Edward had only six months of formal high school before beginning his college education.

Mrs. Lumsdaine (Monika) is a native of Kriens, Switzerland, a town of 10,000 people near Lucerne. She graduated from the Commercial High School for Girls in Lucerne in 1958 and came to America at the invitation of friends, Mr. and Mrs. Arthur P. Langford of Rancho Arnaz, Ventura in 1958.

She began her college career at Ventura College and there met Edward, an Australian-Chinese born in Hong Kong. At 14 he earned passage to the United States by working on a ship for a year and a half. Prior to entering Ventura College, he was a staff sergeant in the U.S. Air Force.

Monika is one of eight students among the New Mexico State College of Arts and Sciences 1,100 students to earn straight A's during the spring semester. She is now a sophomore, majoring in mathematics. Among her talents is flying airplanes—not an active interest now, with marriage and college.

Edward maintained straight A's during the first six-weeks summer session at NMSU and was one of 88 students in the College of Engineering's 1,100-man student body to achieve the spring semester Dean's List. He is a junior, majoring in mechanical engineering.

Monika's parents are Mr. and Mrs. Angelo Amsler of Kriens, Switzerland, while Edward's parents are Mr. and Mrs. Clifford V. Lumsdaine, 396 Wall Street, Ventura.

Ventura friends have received word from the couple that they're expecting a new addition to the family in April.

A photo was included in the article, showing me with a slide rule and Monika pointing to it while holding a pencil over an open notebook. Unfortunately, the newsprint photo does not have a high enough resolution to be digitally reproduced here.

1961 was an enjoyable year of focused learning for both of us. The next year brought a big change as announced by the newspaper article above, for which we thank God. Our lives would never be the same again.

Over the next few years, we were to learn the answer to the question: Is it possible to get a higher education while raising a family? We had no inkling of how this change would impact Monika in particular. She had not given much thought to a possible future career—we viewed her education at this time as a type of insurance policy, in case something happened to me that would prevent me from getting a good-paying job.

CHAPTER ELEVEN

Edward: First Son and First Degree

Both Monika and I took classes in the summer of 1961. To our great joy, Monika had become pregnant. She continued with classes in the fall and took time off in the spring to prepare for the birth. We attended natural childbirth classes together, although the local hospital did not allow fathers in the delivery room.

Monika started labor in mid-April about two weeks before the due date, and our son arrived within four hours. I sent a telegram to her parents the same day. Below is an excerpt from a letter Monika wrote to them a few days later (#144 and translated here from the original German). Communication with her family in those days typically took three weeks before receiving a reply. Hard to imagine with instant communication in the digital age. Definitely a major cultural change!

Liebes Mameli, lieber Papi,

How does it feel, being grandparents? I'm only writing a short letter, so that you don't need to worry about us. Yesterday I was discharged from the hospital. Last night, Andrew had the hiccups, and thus we didn't sleep. I'm very tired.

Last Tuesday I had a touch of stomach flu, but two days later, I felt a lot better. I was about ready to go to bed, when my water broke. Labor pains started immediately, two and a half minutes apart. Edward dashed out of our apartment to the centrally located telephone, and the doctor said I should come to the hospital right away. I didn't even have time to wash my feet, muddy from a bit of gardening that afternoon. My neighbor heard the commotion in our bedroom and asked me if I needed help. She came over to pack my bag.

I was in the labor room about 3 hours, and Edward was with me the entire time. Then I was taken to the delivery room without Edward. I was so tired, all I wanted to do was sleep. So, the doctor gave me some anesthesia. The next thing I heard was that I had a healthy baby boy. There was some problem with expelling the placenta completely, and I was hooked up to an IV line.

In the morning I had a fever, and I was not allowed to hold my little son. He is so cute and a darling, and the first day he was rather sleepy. But when he's unhappy, he can scream at the top of his lungs. We are very happy! I think he looks a bit like me with fair hair and a bit like Edward with somewhat oriental eyes and a flat nose bridge. I'll write more next time. We were so surprised that he arrived two weeks early. The labor pains weren't bad, except for my backache—this came because he was "sunny side up." I still have pain and can hardly sit, walk, or even lie down. The baby came so fast, that I tore and needed stitches.

A million kisses, Monika, Edward, and Andrew

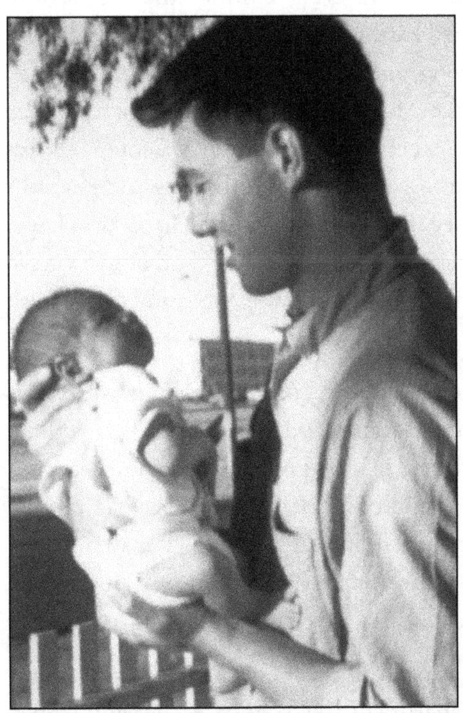

After his birth, the little guy loudly protested being placed in the bassinet—I thought he would wake up the whole hospital. Within a half hour, he managed to wiggle around to where he was lined up in the opposite direction from the other babies in the nursery. At home he was only happy when we placed him in a large crib with open slats all around. No enclosed bassinet for him—he wanted to see all around him.

I felt proud about having my first son, and I looked forward to having a large family. Monika was not quite so enthusiastic after she found how much work it was to care for an infant. She has always been a low-energy person and has been able to accomplish much only by inventing many housekeeping shortcuts. For three months, Monika was treated for postpartum depression. Our active little boy was a challenge for her. How he kept going on a small amount of food and without taking naps puzzled me.

Having a baby brought many changes into our lives. We washed diapers every day, hung them up to dry on the line, and then took them down and folded them almost immediately—they dried quickly in the hot desert sun. We arranged our class schedule so one of us would always be home. Classes were offered six days a week. I had a Monday-Wednesday-Friday schedule, and Monika took Tuesday-Thursday-Saturday classes.

To pay the doctor and hospital bills, we sold our VW Beetle to one of my instructors. We now had to take the bus to the doctor or the supermarket. I began to go to the library in the evening to study because it was impossible to concentrate when a colicky baby cried inconsolably for hours, especially the first six weeks of his life.

We were friends with one couple, Wayne and Roberta Clark, who just accepted us—they truly were colorblind. Roberta and the other ladies from the Baptist Church in nearby Mesilla Park gave Monika a baby shower with many useful baby-care items, clothing, and a little stroller. We were touched by their thoughtfulness to a stranger. Monika and I had not gone to church since arriving in Las Cruces. A few weeks before Andrew was due, Monika was burdened because of the promise we had made to baptize and raise our children Catholic. She went to see the campus priest. His counsel was unexpected—he said that it made no sense to baptize our child now if we did not live the faith. Therefore, we should wait until we were ready to establish a truly Christian home.

Andrew was blond, and this caused an unforeseen problem. His hair was not a surprise to us, knowing that both Monika and my father had been blond as children. However, it caused a lot of talk by people who did not know I was biracial. In addition, my wife would occasionally hear racial slurs made about me which she usually kept to herself, in fear that I might start a fight if the culprits were still within range. Unfortunately, these tensions put a strain on our relationship.

For the summer of 1962, I got a job with Shell Oil Company in Roswell, New Mexico. We sublet our little apartment to a school teacher and loaded up what we needed for the summer into an old clunker I had bought. We left before dawn the day after my last final exam. We drove south to El Paso and then turned east toward Carlsbad. About one hundred miles out of El Paso, the water pump gave out around 7 am. I stopped the car, got out, and lifted the hood to inspect the damage. All of a sudden, I heard an ominous sound and before I could react, I felt something strike my leg. I went back to the driver's seat, sat down, and calmly told Monika, "I think a snake bit me." She looked outside and saw a large rattler with its tongue flicking.

Right then, a truck stopped across the road from us. The driver came over and asked, "Do you need help?" We nodded and pointed to the side of the road. He took one look at the snake, went back to his truck to get a revolver, and shot it in the head. Then he gave me an order, "Roll up your pant leg." He carefully examined my leg and commented, "The rattler missed puncturing your skin—probably because it was still stiff from a cold night."

We breathed a sigh of relief. The truck driver told us, "Just a couple of miles down the road is a garage with a café where a Greyhound bus might stop—you can wait there and flag it down." I asked, "Could you please give us your address?" Later Monika wrote a thank-you note for his help and enclosed a five-dollar bill, which was a lot of money for us. He wrote back, "Over many years of driving my rig and stopping to help people, you were the first to send a thank-you."

I slowly drove us to the garage. Unfortunately, they did not have the right water pump model in stock. The mechanic suggested I buy it in Roswell and bring it back by bus. We decided get breakfast in the café. A pair of unsavory-looking men offered to drive us to where we needed to go. We declined and went outside to wait on the side of the road for the bus. Soon a car passed us that came to a screeching halt. It backed up to where we were sitting. It was a classmate of mine, with his wife. "What are you doing here?" he asked. We explained our predicament. He put his hand under his chin and looked at his wife, explaining, "We're on our way to visit my in-laws. I don't know why we chose this road today—we've always taken a more southerly route before. But now we would like to drive you to Roswell." We gladly accepted and took along as many of our belongings as we could stuff into their trunk.

About a week later, I took a day off from my new job to go back and get the car fixed. The mechanic explained, "You were wise not to go with those two men in the café. Likely, they would have robbed and murdered you, and your bodies would have been dumped or hurriedly buried in the desert."

My summer job was interesting and fun. First, I was a sort of roustabout—I was sent out from the oilfields to a drilling location to pick up core samples. The rednecks working on these rigs did a good amount of kidding "the college boy", but they never called me any racial names. I saw awesome lightning storms. Once while driving, I came close to hitting a cow. It was standing in the middle of the road and blended so well into the grayish-brown landscape, that it was almost invisible. The office staff found I was really good at math, and I was assigned many tasks, including writing a report on seismic testing, for which I received three college credits for undergraduate research.

That summer we lived in a small trailer in someone's backyard, and the crib took up most of the space in the living room. Right then, we decided we would be very unlikely to ever enjoy long trips in a camper—I could barely fit my six-foot-one frame into the kitchen area, bedroom, or tiny shower cubicle. Late in the evening, Monika and I would sit on the little stoop outside to cool off and talk. Once we saw an amazing meteor shower.

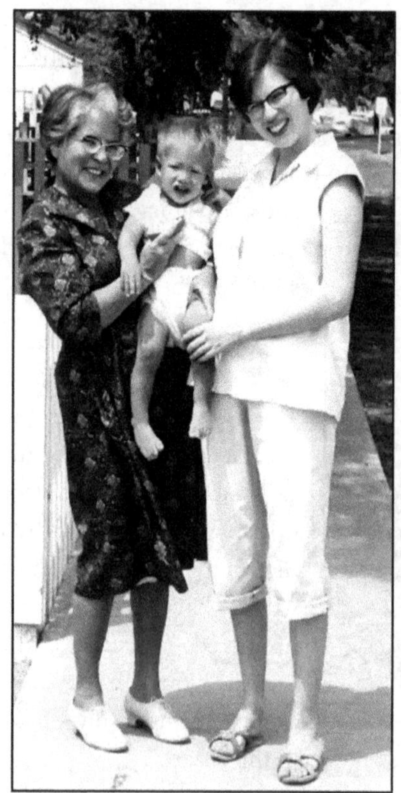

Our car drove well for quite a while, and for the return trip to Las Cruces, I took a chance with the mountain route via Ruidoso and Cloudcroft. Monika enjoyed it very much, as it reminded her of the Swiss Alps.

At the end of January 1963, I met all requirements for my Bachelor of Science degree in mechanical engineering (BSME) with honors. Having done so well, I wanted to keep going—I had developed a real joy of learning and discovering knowledge. I wanted to get into research, and for this I needed more education. I was granted a graduate assistantship in my department at NMSU and began taking courses toward a master's degree.

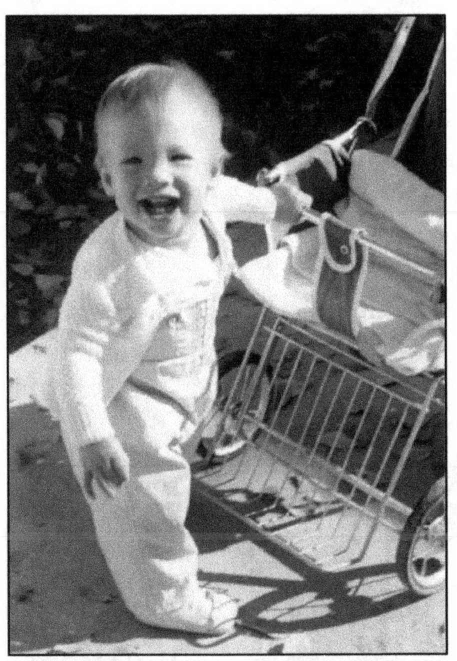

In the spring, my mother-in-law came for an extended visit. Monika was pregnant again and had quite a bit of morning sickness; she was glad to have help with Andrew. Her mother enjoyed caring for and playing with her first grandchild.

Our Andrew was a cheerful and inquisitive little boy, always up for taking a risk. He was good at climbing. As soon as he could walk (at ten months), he tried to escape from our small front yard or the larger yard that separated our barracks. He figured out how to undo the latch at the top of the big double gates. The neighbors were not pleased when Andrew let their children escape out into the street.

Once, while Andrew was playing in our front yard, Monika did some housework inside. She kept the front door open, so she could keep an eye on him through the screen. She was startled when a woman holding Andrew by the hand knocked on the door and asked if she knew to whom the little boy belonged. She had found him walking down the middle of the street, following a bunch of students. Monika was quite embarrassed to have to admit that she was his mother. After that we had to tie the latch of the garden gate shut. This photo shows Andrew outside our screen door with the hobby horse that Monika made for him.

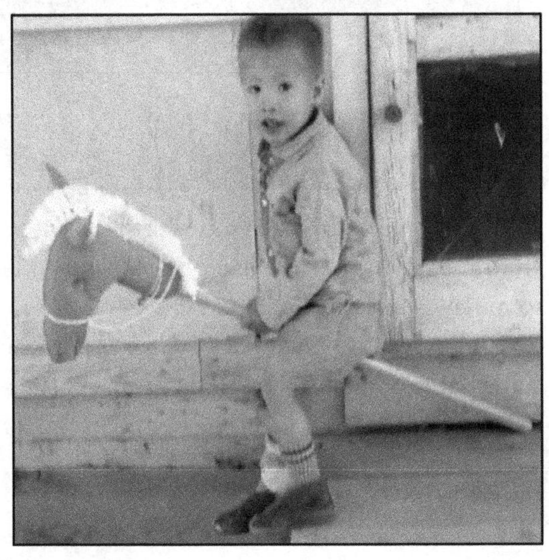

Right after the last final exam in June, we left for California. I had a position as an engineer (GS-7) with the Naval Civil Engineering Lab in Port Hueneme.

We rented a house in Ventura not too far from where my parents lived. The garden had two apricot trees, and little Andrew would spend hours sitting by the trees waiting for ripe fruit to fall while digging in the dirt. Monika made jam for my mother and us. An avocado tree grew there as well, and we liked eating this free fruit, once we discovered the halves tasted best with Worcester sauce poured into the center. My mother fed Andrew special tidbits such as fish eyes, which he relished. The photo shows our son with his two aunts, Milly and Dolly, who came to play with him.

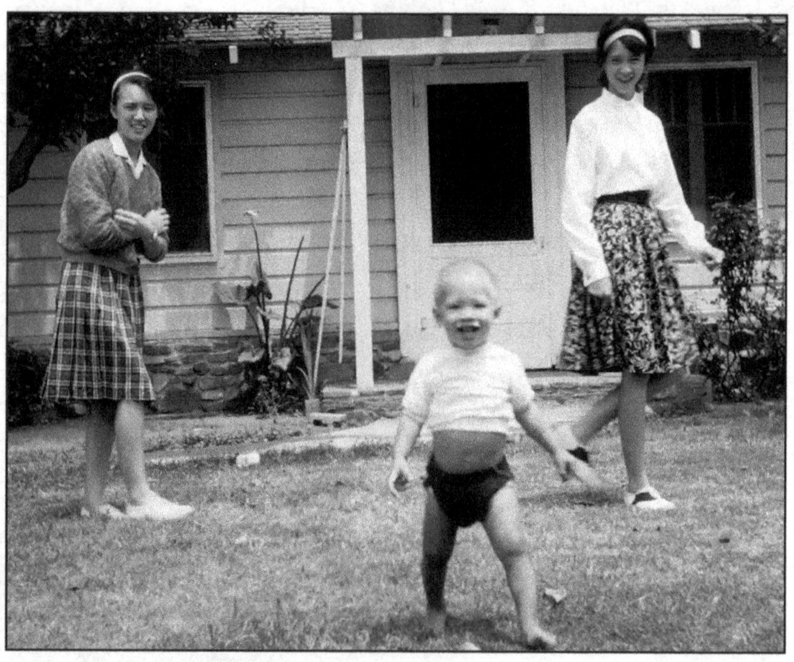

Many a weekend I got roped into playing *mahjong*. I don't think Monika knew the hold this game had on me. She blamed my mother for demanding so much of my time and attention, and I didn't clear up this misconception. One night was traumatic for Monika. Andrew had a high fever, and I didn't come home until they were both asleep. The next day Andrew was diagnosed with bronchitis. It took a while before Monika forgave me.

CHAPTER TWELVE

Edward: A Daughter and Master's Degree

Although I enjoyed the break away from college and the work was easy in Port Hueneme, it was good to be back in Las Cruces after the summer. We had a safe trip despite extreme heat in the desert and a flat tire. We had Andrew immunized with the new measles vaccine when he was 18 months old, together with a dose of gamma globulin to minimize a possible reaction. A week later he got a combined vaccination against tetanus, whooping cough, and diphtheria. Andrew's little friend didn't get the measles vaccine, and his mother had to take off work for three weeks to care for her very sick son.

In early November 1963, our daughter Anne was born. Again, I was not allowed to be present, but Monika said this was an especially easy birth. My newborn daughter was beautiful with peachy skin and fair hair, in contrast to the other babies in the hospital nursery who were red, wrinkled, and had mops of dark hair. About six hours after her birth, I sent my father-in-law a telegram (#194):

Girl 3300 grams born 1:50 am today. Mother and daughter both fine. Ed

Below are some excerpts from Monika's letter (#195) written to her family a few days after giving birth, with more details about this wonderful event.

Around 11 o'clock in the evening, when I started with mild labor pains every five minutes, Edward called the doctor who wanted me to come to the hospital right away. We said good-bye to Andrew at a neighbor's house. The doctor examined me and predicted the baby would come by 5 am. I was resting comfortably, and Edward was reading a magazine. None of the labor pains lasted more than 30 seconds. It was after 1 o'clock when suddenly I got such a strong contraction, it practically lifted me off the bed. I was so surprised. Edward called the nurse who took one look, and I was whisked off to the delivery room. I was wide awake and could watch the whole birth process in a large mirror. No wonder the nurse was in a hurry: I could already see the baby's head. After four pushes, the whole baby suddenly slid out. The stitches this time did not hurt, the placenta came quickly, and I felt great. I think I could have walked home; I was so high on adrenalin. I was unable to sleep that night, even though I was given a sleeping pill, nor all the next day. I was allowed to get up 8 hours after giving birth. The following day I had the usual depression from the hormone shift, but I was allowed to go home.

Anne resembles Andrew but has a rounder face, and everyone marvels how pretty she is. She hardly cries. Andrew likes her. He brings her toys, pets her, and wants to help take care of her when I change her diapers or feed her. I'm thankful that this time I have plenty of breastmilk. Andrew now wants to "go bye-bye" with his daddy all the time, since Edward had taken him along everywhere while I was in the hospital. I'm glad we received dresses for Anne, since I only had boy baby clothes.

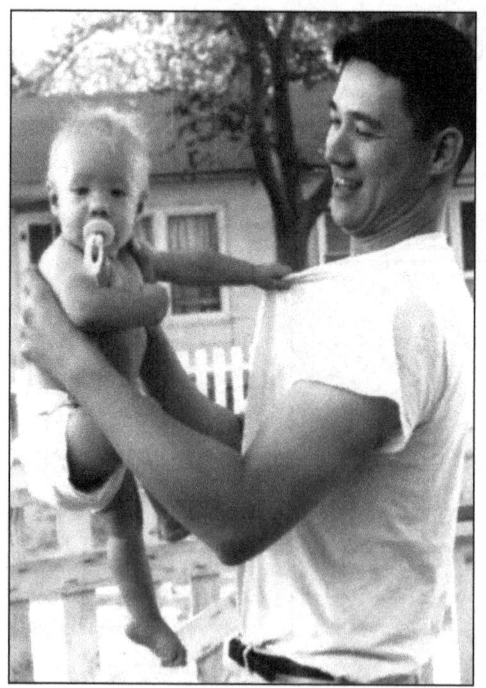

We paid $250 for the delivery, the hospital and the doctor combined, including prenatal care. Ten days later, Monika could report that Andrew was sleeping through the night, and Anne only woke up twice to nurse. This allowed Monika to get more sleep and recover her strength. Anne was a strong little girl. In the photo she held onto my T-shirt for more than twenty minutes and was determined not to let go. Monika wrote about Anne this way:

This child is simply an angel. She is always happy and hardly cries. The day before yesterday, she laughed out loud when Edward was talking to her. She doesn't make fists but has her long fingers stretched out. Edward is naturally very glad to have a little girl. I guessed wrong again and had expected another boy.

To help Monika with housework for a few weeks after Anne's birth, I hired a diaper service as well as a college student for two hours a day. Anne liked to be held, and Monika typed my master's thesis with our daughter on one arm. Anne turned out to be precocious in language development, and we cannot remember when she was not talking. Even from a young age, she was tenacious in pursuing whatever she had in mind. Just like Andrew, she started walking at ten months.

By the end of the spring term in 1964, I had completed the requirements and received my Master of Science in Mechanical Engineering degree. My thesis was concerned with heat transfer in the upcoming field of solar energy. I was proud about having achieved this milestone in my life by earning my own way (and my wife's) without debt, while still helping my parents.

Immediately after the graduation ceremony, we left for California. I returned to the Naval Civil Engineering Lab as a GS-9, and we rented a house in nearby Oxnard.

Again, I was drawn into gambling by playing mahjong on weekends at my mother's, but not as frequently as I had the year before since we lived further away and now had two young children. Monika was not pleased, but her feelings were mixed because the money I won came in handy. One emergency occurred when Andrew fell off his tricycle and dislocated his elbow.

At the end of summer, I was granted a second year of leave from the Naval Civil Engineering Lab, this time with insurance coverage. That was a blessing as Monika became pregnant during the fall, and I did not have to pay for the delivery costs of this child. Today, with the astronomical costs of medical care, it seems incredible that a doctor's visit in those days cost a mere four dollars.

When we returned to Las Cruces, we were able to move into a little house. It was the first one on the corner of the married student village and right across from the agricultural farm and research station. Could we ever smell the animals when the wind blew from the west! Although I had been accepted to doctoral programs both at the University of Washington in Seattle and Michigan State University in Lansing, I felt I simply could not take the risk to go there without an assured income.

At NMSU, I was offered a NASA traineeship, which included a family allowance, so accepting this offer was the only sensible choice. I now spent more and more hours in the office, working on my research and studying instead of at home. I still could not get long stretches of computer time (with punch cards in those days) until after midnight. Monika continued to take a few classes, and I didn't mind watching the children while she was gone for an hour at a time.

There was an incident that still sends chills down my spine when I think about it. As usual I had come home from the office to eat lunch. When Andrew and Anne were done eating, we let them go out to play in the backyard. Monika and I continued to chat while I enjoyed a cup of coffee. Suddenly, we heard a knock on our front screen door. We found a stranger who told us, "Do you know there is a little girl lying behind the car's rear wheel in your driveway?"

I rushed outside and there was our Anne, fast asleep in the shade. We were horrified about what could have happened if I had hurried out of the house, hopped straight into the car, and started to back out as I had been in the habit of doing. We didn't properly thank this stranger. From then on, I tried to remember to always walk around the back of the car before backing out of a driveway. At the time, I attributed the stranger's appearance to luck, but now I know better—our precious daughter had a guardian angel.

Monika's Comments

What is amazing to me now is how little attention we paid to national issues during that time in the early 1960s. We were hardly aware of the many student protests against the Vietnam War all over the US. I vaguely remember that some classmates were gossiping that one of my math professors had gone to El Paso, Texas to participate in a protest. From the culture of 1962, I only remember Bob Dylan's song, "Blowing in the Wind."

A historically significant event occurred in the civil rights movement, when the Reverend Martin Luther King, Jr. delivered his "I Have a Dream" speech in front of the Lincoln Memorial in Washington, DC on August 28, 1963 to about 200,000 people.

However, one event roughly three months later was to us personally unforgettable. Here is how I described it after one week in a letter to my parents (#199 dated 29 November 1963):

To us it seemed as if a family member had died, when we heard about President Kennedy's death. Andrew was playing with his little friend David outside, and I was hanging wash on the line, when David's father came running out of his apartment (which is across from ours). He said that he had just heard from his television that President Kennedy was shot. This was so incredible, and even a week later, it is still hard to grasp. One by one, as all the neighbors returned from their classes, we were gathered in front of Dan's TV, to listen to further news. No one thought about lunch. One could hardly keep from letting tears fall. Even now, flags are still at half-mast. This is simply incredible, though from all indications, L.B. Johnson will be a good president. At least, he is well prepared.

We heard today, that Cape Canaveral was renamed Cape Kennedy! Poor Mrs. Kennedy and her small children! And to top it off, Harvey Oswald, the President's assassin, was murdered, so the truth and motive will never see the light of day.

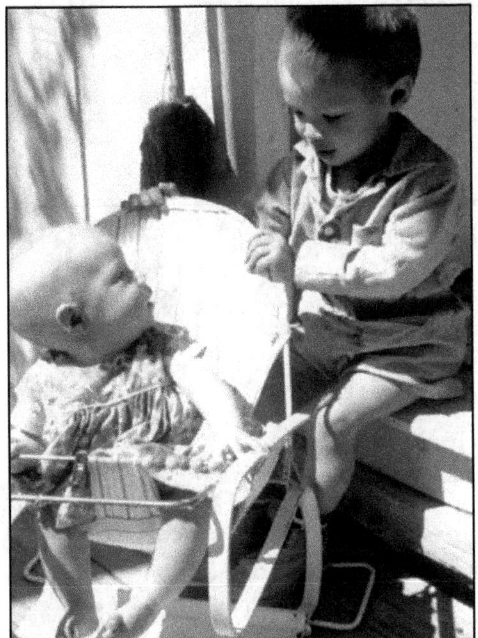

Andrew loved his new sister and did not want anyone else to touch or hold her besides us. He learned how to ride a tricycle on his own. Because he was talking in one-syllables, he called Anne "bee" instead of baby. So, she soon got a nickname, "honeybee." I felt well after her birth, and that Thanksgiving I cooked a 21-pound turkey. I also baked two pumpkin pies and no longer needed an afternoon nap.

I enjoyed the two years we lived in the little house. This area had paved sidewalks which were a safe place for children to ride their tricycles. The house had a lawn in the backyard, and I dug a flowerbed where I grew cosmos and zinnias of amazing size. I still remember the fun Andrew and Anne had playing hide and seek among the bedsheets on the clothesline. On the other hand, I also remember a very large black spider on my "baby bump" when I glanced down in the midst of taking clothes off the line one evening. I reacted instantly by brushing it off—no time to scream or call for help.

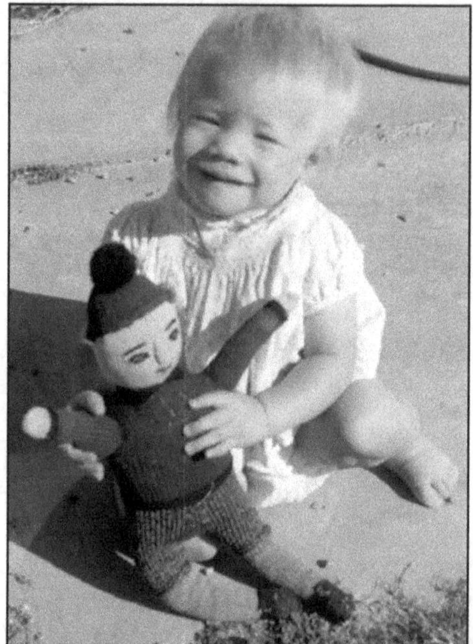

In the photo above, Anne is holding *Peterli,* the knit doll my mother made for me when I was a small child. Now, retired in our apartment, I still have that doll. At 80 years old it needs repair and more stuffing. It has a red cap and red pullover.

The photo at right shows the concrete block wall surrounding our little house. We bought a large wooden plank and leaned it against the wall to help Anne and Andrew reach the top to perch there safely. We had no idea what adventures awaited us in our last year at NMSU.

CHAPTER THIRTEEN

Edward: Second Son and More Degrees

Monika found a letter dated May 14, 1965 that she sent to her family (#236). It gives a glimpse of our plans for what we had hoped to be our last year at New Mexico State University.

Liebes Mameli, lieber Papi, liebes Lili:

Thank you so much for your letters. We've been so busy, I have only a few minutes for writing. My French term paper is finally done, with the oral exam scheduled for next week. Then I have to study some German for an exam between now and the start of the summer term on the topic, "The Modern German Drama." These two items will count as the equivalent of two courses. Then I'm registered for government and chemistry for the eight-week summer session. With six courses in the fall, I'll be all done with my studies.

It will certainly be a big help when Lili comes, because I'll have five hours of classes three days a week. I'll be free in the spring to help Edward with his doctoral dissertation, and if necessary, to do some part-time work like paper grading for extra income. Edward thinks that at the latest by the end of next summer, we would leave here.

Andrew and Anne are looking forward to getting a brother or sister soon. It is so hot, and I can hardly walk; this child is situated very low. We'll have a helper for the household again, and Andrew might be going to kindergarten. Then we'll have time off from August 10 to the middle of September to take it easy for a while.

Our third child, Alfred, was born in early June 1965, and we had quite a scare. I had to rush Monika to the hospital when she started to bleed heavily in the middle of the night. Fortunately, the bleeding stopped, and the baby's heartbeat remained steady. Jacqueline Kennedy, the wife of the American President, had lost a child due to premature separation of the placenta—no wonder we were frightened. Monika was upset that yet again I was not allowed in the delivery room. She brought her camera to the hospital to take pictures. She wrote a long letter to her parents soon after the birth (#238):

Exactly five hours ago, the little guy was born. When Edward comes to visit this afternoon, we'll make the final decision to name him Alfred. He looks like Andrew did at birth, except that he is almost bald, with just a bit of blond fuzz.

I'm feeling well and will be able to get up soon. But mostly I'm resting after all the recent excitement. Two days ago, I had false labor pains all day; then yesterday, I had few pains, although my tummy would feel very hard. I did some serious house cleaning. By evening I was very tired, mostly from all that waiting. I went to sleep around 10 p.m. I woke up about three hours later from a strong contraction. When I discovered that I was bleeding heavily, Edward rushed me to the hospital. He called his friend and fellow doctoral student, Mr. Fang, to babysit.

The nurse in the hospital found that the baby had a strong heartbeat; however, the doctor could not be located for about an hour. His substitute advised not to do any prep but to keep everything ready for an emergency caesarian section. What a busy place—we were five women waiting to give birth. My doctor delivered two babies; then I had a few strong contractions and was wheeled into the stand-by delivery room. Two strong contractions followed, and the baby was born. Since I was flat on my back as ordered, I couldn't see if I aimed or focused the camera correctly, but I hope I have a few good snapshots of the newborn. I got a terrible cramp in my right leg and foot. Finally, the doctor answered my question: 'Why did I bleed so heavily earlier." He said an edge of the placenta detached prematurely in a small area. Edward and I were relieved that all ended well. He predicted we would have a boy, and he was right again.

I was thankful I didn't have much pain and did not need any anesthesia, just a few stitches. I was ravenous for my breakfast and so thirsty, I've already had six glasses of water. There are a few after-pains, but otherwise I feel fine. Alfred is almost the same size as the other two children, 3350 g. But now I'm sleepy and need to take a nap.

We heard from the doctor the next day that the umbilical cord was pressed against the side of the large head of our son during the delivery, creating a potential emergency. It turned out that the cord had been wrapped around the baby's neck in a double loop. Monika had glimpsed the cord but couldn't clearly see what was happening because the doctor's hands were in the way. She was not surprised; she felt this active baby had done quite a number of somersaults in the womb.

It took several weeks before Alfred's crying didn't sound like mere mouse squeaks, but otherwise there were no other detrimental effects, for which we were grateful. For the first few weeks, he would fall asleep while nursing and then cry for more food an hour or two later. Temperamentally, he was a serious baby who was content to sit and watch his siblings play. Therefore, it was a surprise when he also started to walk at ten months.

Two days after Alfred's birth, Monika's chemistry class started. This was a freshman course she had postponed to this summer. It had a three-hour lab in the afternoon, which was exhausting. During her senior year, Monika mostly picked easy courses such as German and French literature. These she could do while staying at home with the children, by writing reports instead of having to attend classes. Since I was close to completing my work for the doctorate, I encouraged her to get her math degree before we left NMSU. I saw this as insurance in case she might have to help support our family.

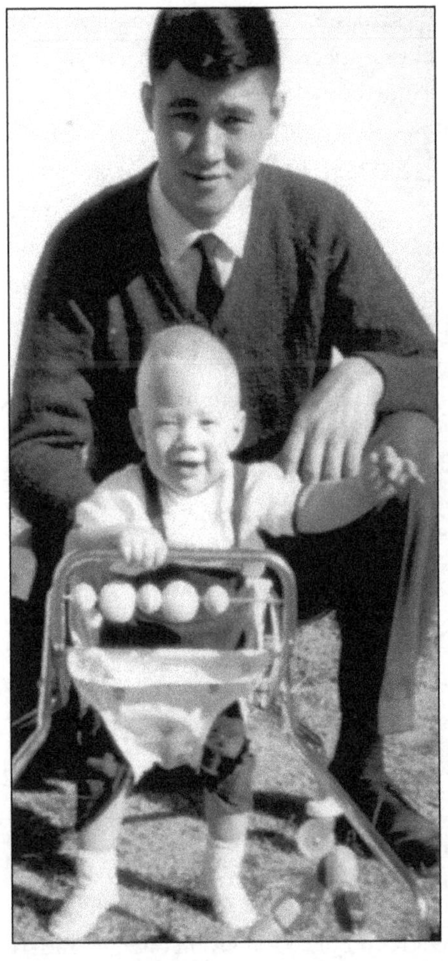

When Alfred was about four months old, Monika came down with a severe case of bronchitis. She had to be in an oxygen tent in the hospital for several days. I had a crying baby on my hands who refused to drink from a bottle. It was a whole day before he was hungry enough to take formula and then only after it was warmed up to just the right temperature.

If we could do this over, we would put Monika's health and caring for our children ahead of her getting her degree. I also want to mention that since Monika's first pregnancy, I stopped smoking at home. She had severe morning sickness with each child, and the smell of smoke made it worse. Also, with us living in those old, wooden barracks, I worried about the fire hazard related to my smoking. I wanted my family to be safe.

We did not have much time or money for recreation. We made an occasional outing to White Sands National Monument or a Mexican restaurant in Mesilla Park. We remember going to the drive-in movie theatre once to see *Ben Hur* with the children sleeping in the back of our station wagon. Basically, we had a simple life centered on our studies, with few distractions. We did belong to a science book club, and our book shelves made of planks and cement blocks steadily grew.

In early December 1965, I successfully passed the written comprehensive examination for my Doctor of Science degree (later changed by the University to PhD). Monika's sister Lili came to visit for several weeks (shown in the photo holding Anne). Monika was thankful for Lili's timely help, because she was trying to finish her courses and recover from her illness. In later years, Lili would comment how hard she had to work while living with us. However, she did take time off for travel to California and skiing in Taos. She enjoyed playing with baby Alfred, dressing up Anne in a little Swiss costume, and buying Andrew a drum.

I was depressed that winter. My research and dissertation subject for my doctorate involving fluid flow through various ducts was no longer exciting and was not at all what I had envisioned. It got so bad I was ready to quit. Monika encouraged me to persist and get on with my dissertation. Even today I have trouble buckling down to writing when a topic bores me, so this was very difficult. Only the thought of getting it done to move on to an interesting and well-paying job kept me going.

In February 1966, I was invited to present a research paper at a conference in Boston. I decided to drive and take my family along. I was glad that Monika could take an occasional turn at the wheel so I could nap. I had finally taught her how to drive a car with an automatic transmission when Alfred was six weeks old. Monika had an appointment at MIT, where she had applied for a position in their graduate school. But with only two openings for over one hundred applicants, she was turned down. She had two strikes against her: being a mother with three children and not having taken the most advanced modern math courses. Secretly I was glad. I shudder to think what would have happened if my wife had gone on to pursue a full-time professional career while our children were young.

Both of us also interviewed with General Electric and Westinghouse. She got an offer from Westinghouse; I got one from GE's Missile and Space Division. If we had job offers from the same company, we might have been tempted to rethink our decision about her not working outside the home.

In the spring, Monika edited and typed my dissertation on an electric typewriter, with seven carbon copies. I had to pass two foreign language exams. Chinese did not count in fulfilling the foreign language requirements for the doctorate, but I passed the French exam without studying and the German exam with extensive coaching from Monika. Fortunately, I did not have to know how to speak the languages well; I only had to have a rudimentary understanding of the grammatical structures to be able to read and translate technical material with the help of a dictionary. Monika's German professor told me, "Your German is atrocious. I will pass you, but you have to promise to let Monika do any translations that you need in the future." I believe I was able to finish my doctorate in only two years because I did not need to take any language courses.

I now got serious about my job search. I had two invitations for site visits. The two experiences were as different as night and day. I flew to Seattle where I was wined and dined. Boeing gave me the royal treatment on plant tours and introduced me to key people at two or three research centers. In my new dark blue wool-silk suit I felt comfortable talking with everyone and giving a presentation on my research work. I never doubted during the entire process that I would get a favorable job offer. It seemed they needed me more than I needed them, and I felt astonished and gratified that the world-renowned Boeing Company wanted my services!

For the interview in San Diego, I decided to drive and take my family with me. This interview was with a research laboratory associated with Shell Oil. I had been nominated by my former supervisor in Roswell, and they had called me. This turned out to be a very strange experience. Subtly, I felt I was being put down when people left and right were pointed out to me as having degrees from Cal Tech, Stanford, MIT, and similar prestigious institutions. There was little rapport between my areas of competence and what they were looking for. During dinner with a technical staff group, I was mostly ignored—some of the engineers in the group even started to read newspapers. I left as soon as I could, and I felt depressed for a while after this interview. But Monika and the children enjoyed their time on the beach at La Jolla while I was in meetings, and we visited my parents in Ventura.

In May I received a telegram with a job offer from Boeing. A formal letter providing more details about the position soon followed. It didn't take much time or discussion with Monika before I decided to accept. I asked my advisor, Dr. Milan Cobble, to please read my dissertation quickly and schedule the final examination, the defense of my doctoral research work. Instead, he unexpectedly decided it was not right to get a doctorate in only two years, and he let my dissertation sit on his desk unread and unsigned for weeks, causing me to miss graduating with the class of 1966. He finally convened the examination committee for June 10. Professor Cobble had had other doctoral students who had worked with him for several years, so his reluctance to let me go early is understandable.

We had invited my parents to the graduation ceremony for Saturday, May 28, at 8 pm. My parents, my sister Maria, and other family members all came to Las Cruces to cheer for Monika who was at the head of the procession into Memorial Stadium. and they saw her receive a gold medal as the top university graduate (of 550 students). I was very proud of her and again counted myself very lucky. Of course, my parents were disappointed that I was not marching in the graduation parade.

I was also proud of myself. I had put my wife through school as well as myself, and I was about to graduate with only a modest amount of debt. Also, for the entire time as a student, I had faithfully continued to support my mother. I don't think my parents really appreciated or understood what I had sacrificed and accomplished.

I clearly remember June 10, the day I defended my dissertation in Jett Hall, Room 106. The meeting started at 3:30 pm, and the weather was stormy. At first the examination went well, and I was able to answer the questions of the six faculty members on my committee to their satisfaction. Then Professor Shouman, the expert in fluid flow, asked a question that simply stumped me. Suddenly, there was a loud thunderclap, and the lights went out. The faculty members started to speculate about what might have happened.

When the power came back on in half an hour, Dr. Shouman had forgotten his question. I passed. Monika told me later that the transformer on a utility pole right next to our house had been hit by lightning. New Mexico State University sent me a letter stating the official date of my degree, now listed as Ph.D, was July 30, 1966. Since the university had only one graduation ceremony per year, I could have received my doctoral hood in the spring of 1967. However, by then I lived too far away to bother.

We sold most of our thrift-store furnishings to other students. A moving company came to pick up the few items that we wanted to take to Seattle. Monika finished loading our car during a rain shower and got drenched and chilled. We made a last round through the empty but spic-and-span house, bundled the kids into the car, and were finally on our way. We didn't have to rush on this trip and decided to see the Grand Canyon. By the time we reached Flagstaff, Monika had a sore throat and high fever, and she was too dizzy to really enjoy the amazing scenery from the rim of the canyon.

We stayed in Ventura with my family while Monika recovered. The photo of Alfred was snapped in their front yard. Then we drove on to San Francisco and across the Golden Gate. We continued up the Oregon coast, took leisurely detours past rainforests and arrived in Seattle a day or two before my starting date with Boeing. Everything was beautiful!

Leaving Las Cruces was easy—we left no close friends behind. Monika was looking forward to new furniture in a nice house near the mountains and the sea. The children were looking forward to us having a television set. And I was looking forward to my job as a research engineer at $14,000 per year—I was eager to start a new adventure as a professional. I strongly felt I had accomplished a milestone. I had a "full house": three children and both my wife and I had completed our formal education and had earned degrees with honors in respected fields. This time the Golden Gate represented an open path to success in a professional career!

I had achieved a good education—an important component of the American Dream—and I was able to take care of my family. Now it was time to put my learning into practice as an engineer. I was well poised for this new journey. But I did not yet know who I needed to thank for our blessings.

Monika's Comments

The five and a half years in Las Cruces flew by quickly. We were always very busy studying during the regular semesters. Starting with 1962, we would rush off to Edward's summer job location right after the last final exam. In hindsight, there is one thing I would do differently: take time to enjoy more moments for recreation and for sightseeing side trips, even if it meant foregoing a day's pay.

Academically, the only course I ever dropped was modern math. None of the other courses were real challenges except Electricity and Magnetism. I earned an A, but feel I just lucked out because I didn't really understand the subject. I was the only female in the class, and the guys didn't always do their homework. One day Professor Duncan asked us to write the completed homework problem on the blackboard. I was the only one who was able to do it, so that gave me some brownie points. As luck would have it, only those topics I reviewed were on the final exam, and I also noticed that one of the illustrations in the textbook had been reverse printed, and thus the vectors in the picture were wrong.

The one thing I vividly remember from the English literature class taught by Professor Hartmann was her enthusiasm for authors who created a fictional character that would "come alive" as an icon, like Frodo Baggins from *The Lord of the Rings* by J.R.R. Tolkien. This story grew to be an all-time favorite of mine and I later read it aloud to our children. I still enjoy reading the story and watching the three-part movie in the extended version with our grandchildren.

I almost did not graduate on time because I was short two physical education credits. Edward's physical education requirements were waived because he was a veteran. I got deferrals either for pregnancy or nursing a baby. I had to submit a special petition for a waiver. I reasoned that chasing after three preschoolers was surely enough daily exercise for anyone, and I did have more than the minimum credits required for graduation. I sighed with relief when the waiver was granted.

I was invited to join the honor society Phi Kappa Phi, and as the top-ranking senior student, I had the position of vice-president of the chapter. The only responsibility this entailed was organizing one of the monthly meetings. Since I had always wanted to visit the university's observatory on nearby A-mountain, I chose this as an evening excursion for the chapter. It turned out to be very interesting and appreciated by everyone. This was my first experience in a leadership position. The fact that Edward was also a member made this even more enjoyable.

Halfway through my courses at NMSU, the requirements for a math degree were changed with two computer math courses added. But students already enrolled could choose to graduate under the old rules. Because I did not want to add two more courses before I could graduate, I chose the old option. In hindsight, this was a big mistake. When I interviewed for jobs, the first question invariably asked was, "What computer courses have you taken?" In the future when I had a chance to talk with students, I would always urge them to take every opportunity to learn about new developments and new technology!

How did the different cultures—Chinese, Swiss, and American—affect our parenting? How did the way we were brought up influence the way we were raising our children? Edward and I did not want to use our parents as role models. Our parents did not have good role models themselves. In Switzerland, starting from birth, children were raised according to a strict schedule. My father, brought up in an orphanage, did not believe that daughters should be hugged. Neither Edward's father nor mother expressed affection toward him—a cultural influence? His father was absent through no fault of his own for much of Edward's growing-up years. His mother, overwhelmed with eight children in dismal circumstances, left him to fend for himself or disciplined him severely.

Thus, both Edward and I were on our own. I had never been around a baby and had to "learn how to swim by being cast into the water." Dr. Benjamin Spock's *Baby and Child Care* book (which was widely accepted in the American culture in the 1960s) helped us with its mainly common-sense approach, although it was criticized as being too permissive with "feeding-on-demand." We tried our best to be responsible parents. For example, we used a safety harness in our car for the small children until they could use the regular safety belts. This was long before it became mandated by law.

Life was simple for us then. Were these the good old days? We didn't have much beyond the bare necessities in furniture, and I sewed most of my clothing and that of the children. I also cut everyone's hair. We did buy a few quality toys like building blocks. I made large and small stuffed animals which lead to many hours of imaginative play for the children. We acquired a huge tire and filled it with sand. We also bought tricycles and a wagon. Balls, however, did not last long because of the thorny weeds in the lawn. Since reading were important to us, we subscribed to two children's magazines and a children's book club.

One event from 1966 in our family was the death of my maternal grandmother, Josephine Dériaz, at age 94 in Baulmes, Switzerland. We were able to visit her grave there in 1971. See Appendix 2 for details about my family tree.

With the move to Seattle, things for our family were about to alter drastically. Because I grew up mainly in a rural landscape, I've always been happy in that kind of environment. Although Edward was looking forward to working and living in Seattle, I found myself wondering how city life would affect our children and me. What I did not anticipate was being entirely uprooted, "cast adrift" and socially isolated. Since my studies were completed at this time, I was without goals. Edward would have his challenging and interesting work and colleagues to talk to, whereas I missed his frequent presence during the day and the time we had spent studying together and discussing daily happenings.

I knew a big change was ahead, but I could not foresee how difficult my life in Seattle would turn out to be and how the dark winter days with its "dark shadows" and depression would affect me. Now looking back, perhaps I needed this time without many distractions to learn how to be an attentive mother to my children and to appreciate what was to come next in our future. Although our formal education had ended, the expansion of our family was not yet complete, and three surprising changes occurred in my life within the next three years.

CHAPTER FORTEEN

Monika: Citizenship, a Baby, and Spiritual Life

Several events affected our life during the year we lived in Seattle. Edward's job of working on the SST (supersonic transport) was canceled, and he was assigned to research on airplane noise reduction, a much less challenging subject. We were unable to buy a house in a neighborhood we liked due to existing racial discrimination. I was in a car accident; I took a self-defense class at the YMCA; I had surgery and spent several painful days in a dark hospital. The highlight for me was becoming a naturalized US citizen in May 1967! Now I could vote! In Switzerland, women did not get to vote until 1971.

Then Edward applied for a job as an assistant professor at several universities. He accepted the first offer, sight unseen, at South Dakota State University in Brookings, a small town in the Midwest, where we found a cozy house to buy. Neighbors welcomed us with fresh corn and apple pie, and we were invited to a small Wesleyan-Methodist church by the pastor and a pair of Sunday school teachers. No surprise that we soon felt at home in our new community. For our children, we built a huge sandbox and set up a jungle gym in the middle, with lots of space for them to play with their new friends.

Forty years since they met on the sailboat, my parents came to visit us in our new location and very much enjoyed their only grandchildren. In 1971, we took a trip to Europe and stayed with them in Switzerland. I remember Alfred was six years old at that time, and we had Eurail passes to also travel to England, France, Italy, and Holland.

In Brookings, Edward and I learned an unfamiliar skill, shoveling mountains of snow, and all of us had to get used to very cold temperatures in the winter. But the first focus of this chapter is the birth of our third son, which completed our family and happened in a more family-friendly way than the births in New Mexico. This child was due at the end of November 1968. That Thanksgiving I felt I was the stuffed turkey. Because winters in South Dakota can bring fierce blizzards, Edward learned about delivering a baby at home just in case.

Finally, on a beautiful, sunny morning, Arnold was born in the small hospital a few blocks from our house. Edward was allowed to be present for this miracle, the birth of one of his children. It went smoothly and very quickly. He was surprised at the casual banter between the doctor, attending nurse, and me. It wasn't the dramatic event often depicted in movies, as described in the letter (#326) I sent to my parents in early December. I am amazed how many details I have forgotten in the half-century since. I'm glad my daughter Anne has archived my letters.

Lieber Papi, liebes Mami,

You've heard the news from the telegram that Edward sent, but here is more information about our newest son's birth. Around three in the morning I woke up with labor pains about five minutes apart. Edward called my friend from our church, Elois Palmer. She lived nearby and had offered to come and stay with our children no matter what time of day or night, for which we were very grateful. Then Edward took me to the hospital. By six o'clock I could hardly stand it, because the worst of the pain was in my back—for which the breathing and relaxation exercises I had practiced were useless. The nurse checked me frequently, but didn't think anything would happen soon. Suddenly I called out, "The baby is coming." Fortunately, the elderly doctor on call appeared at that moment. My regular doctor was out of town for Thanksgiving, but he had left a note with my paperwork that I had very quick deliveries with my previous three children.

It took only minutes to get me to the delivery room and for Edward to put on a face mask, cap and sterile gown. Dr. Tank broke the water, and the baby's head was born immediately. The doctor grumbled that I didn't need to push so hard, as if one could help it. Then I saw why the back pains— this was another sunny-side up baby, and the back of his head had pushed on my spine. He already cried the moment his head appeared. Then with the next tremendous contraction, the entire baby was born. The doctor was not pleased that it happened so fast, since I again got a large tear which he quickly sewed up. The

placenta came right after this, and we had to hurry, because the delivery room was needed for another woman.

I was brought to a beautiful room facing the rising sun. For an hour, Edward could stay with me and our little boy who was already sucking his thumb. He resembles all three of his siblings and especially has Annie's long fingers and toes. I got my breakfast and could rest a while, then the other mother with her boy baby joined me in this room.

The next day it snowed, and I had the usual bout of depression from the hormone shift; I couldn't even keep breakfast down (and both of us mothers cried a lot that day). The next day I felt much better, and late in the afternoon of the fourth day Arnold and I were allowed to go home. There was great rejoicing from the children!

To our surprise, Arnold weighted over 8 pounds! Here, the doctor had not been concerned about my weight gain early in the pregnancy, so I was not put on a restricted diet. Arnold is a very strong little guy. He is starting to cry, so I need to close.

Write again soon. Greetings from all of us, Monika

Anne was at first disappointed; she had expected a little sister. But she was happy once she saw her new baby brother. I guessed wrong again, for the fourth time. But God knew best!

In 1969, we remember two events: Apollo 11 landed on the moon in July, with Neil Armstrong and Buzz Aldrin taking their first steps there "for mankind." And to our surprise, Arnold started to walk at about that time.

We were visiting family in California, and below is a snapshot of Ed's parents thirty-seven years after they met in Shanghai, having fun with their grandchildren Alfred and Arnold. Grandma was babysitting Arnold, so we could take the older children to Knott's Berry Farm and Disneyland.

A few months after Arnold's birth, God blessed me with a different new birth, which changed my life forever. I want to use the rest of the chapter to describe how this came about and its eternal consequences.

When we moved to Brookings, South Dakota (after a year in Seattle), we were invited to attend a friendly church. What I noticed almost right away was the happy singing of hymns and choruses. Also, the people lived by what they believed—they were not mere Sunday Christians. Every few weeks or so the pastor gave an "evangelistic" altar call, and when I felt one was due, we'd skip church attendance that Sunday.

By the spring of 1969, during an altar call, I felt that God wanted me to respond. I knew I needed Him—as a mother of now four children, with the oldest barely seven years old, I felt overwhelmed. However, I was trapped in the pew, the invitation hymn ended, and the opportunity passed.

I had a very uncomfortable week, being under conviction by the Holy Spirit. The following Sunday was Mother's Day. Pastor called all the mothers to the front of the sanctuary for a special prayer and blessing. Then, before dismissing us, he said, "Is there a mother here, who would like to receive Jesus Christ as her Savior?" How merciful God was—now I stood already at the altar, where Pastor Strand prayed for me.

The next day I met with him in his office. He explained what was happening to me. I now was an adopted child of God through the sacrifice of Jesus Christ, my Savior and Lord, since I invited Him into my heart. He forgave all my sins (past, present and future). Now, through the presence of the Holy Spirit, I had a new heart and a renewed mind more like Christ's.

This decision radically changed my life and gave me strength, peace and joy. I remember that spring time—the greens of the grass and the blooming fruit trees were brighter than I had ever noticed before. One immediate sign of a change in me was that I stopped watching the soap opera *Dark Shadows* to which I had become addicted while in Seattle.

I know I am just a pilgrim on this earth and have a heavenly home with God when I die. In 1971, when we made our trip to Europe, I gave a talk with slides to a women's group at a church in Pratteln, at the invitation of my pen-pal Henriette. Then I did the same at a reunion with the Amsler clan. Through these slides of beautiful US landscapes coupled with Bible verses, I tried to explain clearly how we can find the way to heaven by faith. Below is a brief summary of the steps, because my deepest prayer for my family is that we will all be joyfully reunited in heaven with God for all eternity. As you read through these steps, imagine that I am speaking to you directly, heart to heart.

How to Become a Christian and Find Peace with God

At each step, think about what the quoted Bible verses ***in bold italics*** are saying to you. Read them to yourself, aloud!

1. We cannot have eternal life and be in heaven without God's forgiveness, because sin separates us from God. It is impossible for a holy God to allow sin into heaven. However, every person is a sinner.

   For all have sinned and fall short of the glory of God (Romans 3:23). For the wages of sin is death, but the gift of God is eternal life in Christ Jesus our Lord (Romans 6:23).

2. So, how can a sinful person enter heaven, when God allows no sin there?

   In him [Jesus Christ] we have redemption through his blood, the forgiveness of sins, in accordance with the riches of God's grace that he lavishes on us with all wisdom and understanding (Ephesians 1:7).

3. Forgiveness is available for all, but it is not automatic.

   For God so loved the world that he gave his one and only Son, that whoever believes in him shall not perish but have eternal life (John 3:16).

4. Therefore, we must turn and repent from sin and self. Do turn to Christ; trust Him only!

   But unless you repent, you will all perish (Luke 13:3).

   If you confess with your mouth "Jesus is Lord," and believe in your heart that God raised him from the dead, you will be saved (Romans 10:9).

5. Heaven is eternal life. Jesus offers eternal life here and eternal life hereafter. He lives!

   "I have come that they may have life and have it in abundance" (John 10:10). "If I go away and prepare a place for you, I will come back and take you to be with me, that you also may be where I am" (John 14:3). "I am the way and the truth and the life. No one comes to the father except through me" (John 14:6).

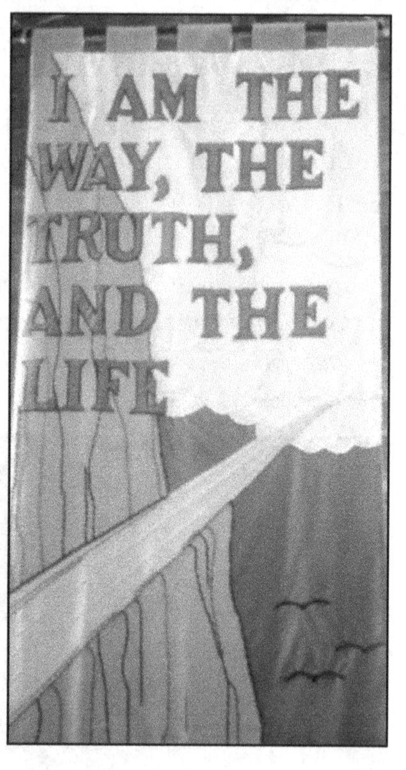

6. He can do this because He was born into our world to die for us, and then He rose from the dead.

   But God demonstrates his own love for us in this: while we were still sinners, Christ died for us (Romans 5:8).

7. We can receive Jesus Christ into our life through prayer:

   "Dear Jesus, I believe that you died on a cross for my sins and that you rose from the grave. I now ask you to forgive me of my sins and to save my soul. Amen."

   Your assurance that Jesus has answered your prayer is this:

   "I tell you the truth, whoever hears my word and believes him who sent me has eternal life and will not be condemned; he has crossed over from death to life" (John 5:24).

My trust in Jesus Christ as my Redeemer has made all the difference in my life; He is my sure hope, my strength, and my comforter. He is my rock, my fortress, my deliverer, and my shield (Psalm 18:1-2). He is there for me in hard times:

The Lord is my shepherd; I shall not be in want. He makes me lie down in green pastures; He leads me beside quiet waters. He

restores my soul. He guides me in paths of righteousness for his name's sake. Even though I walk through the valley of the shadow of death, I will fear no evil, because you are with me; your rod and your staff, they comfort me... Surely goodness and mercy will follow me all the days of my life, and I will dwell in the house of the Lord forever (Psalm 23: 1-4, 6).

God's Word, the Bible, has been my guide and teaches me more about Him, as does having fellowship with other believers in my church family. I have been blessed through attending Bible-believing churches wherever we have lived.

But these are written that you may believe that Jesus is the Christ, the Son of God, and that by believing you may have life in His name (John 20:31).

As for God, his way is perfect; the word of the Lord is flawless (Psalm 18:30). The word of the Lord is right and true; he is faithful in all he does (Psalm 33:4).

And the moment we receive Christ, we are given a precious gift, the Holy Spirit, to teach us to understand His Word, to lead us, to give assurance that we have been adopted into God's family. I thank God for all the adventures and journeys in my life, for my dear husband, loving children, and precious grandchildren, as well as for the beauty of the earth that we can see in His creation. Above all, I thank Him for sending His Son to die for me, so I can live with Him forever.

Difficult times have taught me more about God's faithfulness to me than when everything is going well—I found Him to be my comfort and strength in all circumstances.

Rejoice in the Lord always. Do not be anxious about anything, but in everything, by prayer and petition, with thanksgiving, present your requests to God. And the peace of God, which transcends all understanding, will guard your hearts and your minds in Christ Jesus (Philippians 4:4,6-7).

God was with me when I found that I had breast cancer a few years ago, and more recently, when I broke my right femur and had to have a hip replacement. I have seen God's continuing work in Edward's life in his battle and recovery from gambling addiction, as described in the Postscript. I can truly say, in the last lines of the song, *"All I have Is Christ"* (by Jordan Kauflin, Sovereign Grace Music):

Father, use my ransomed life in any way you choose.
And let my song forever be, my only boast is you.
Hallelujah! All I have is Christ. Hallelujah! Jesus is my life.

If you have made a humble commitment to follow Jesus, do so in writing. There may come times in the future, when Satan will confuse you, or difficulties (or other people) will lead you to doubt. Or you may have memory loss coming on with old age. Whatever the circumstances, the written document will assure you and help you remember the day you started your eternal relationship with your Savior and Lord Jesus Christ. I would like to suggest a good place to do this—write and sign it in the front of your Bible (with the date when you made your commitment to follow Jesus). Then be strengthened by attending a Bible-believing church and joining a small Bible study and prayer group.

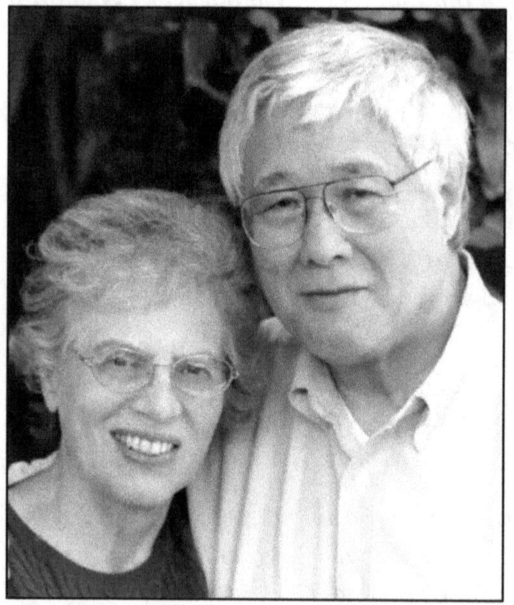

May the truth of God's Words and His presence in your life bless you in the coming years and forever!

In the lengthy Postscript, we are summarizing the rest of the amazing story of what God has done in our lives from 1967 to 2021.

Our daughter took this special photo of us in 2012.

POSTSCRIPT

Edward: Career Moves and Raising Our Children (1967-1992)

Main core values in the Chinese culture come from Confucianism. They focus on self-improvement, morality and education. Once I had completed my education, self-improvement became encompassing and I became a workaholic until I began my part-time retirement in 2013. A sense of pride was also involved, as was morality. My thought was always that I showed my love for my family by giving them nice housing and a good education; they never had to fend for themselves like I had to do in my youth. For example, I was not satisfied with just being a research engineer at Boeing. Soon I took on an additional job, teaching engineering dynamics in the evening at Seattle University, with the excuse that we needed the money. Pride was involved as well. I thought to myself: *"Look at me: I got kicked out of primary school by the Jesuits, and now I am a professor at a Jesuit University!"*

Then I decided to become a faculty member at South Dakota State University, sight unseen. During the fall of 1971 at a men's retreat held by our church, I accepted Jesus Christ as my Savior. In the preceding years, I had read a lot about different religions but had remained an agnostic. My decision to become a "born-again Christian" was primarily motivated by the change I had observed in Monika. I knew she was very intelligent, and thus I was willing to take the gamble and try this conversion as well. But my spiritual growth was at a snail's pace compared to Monika's, with many ups and downs—I was hedging my bets instead of making a total commitment.

Then we moved to Knoxville, where within a year I became one of the youngest full professors in the college of engineering at the University of Tennessee. The racial climate had changed so much since the 1950s that I was no longer concerned about discrimination. I was able to obtain research funding and built a respectable publication record about my work.

My sister, Maria, called that our mother was in critical condition in the hospital due to a large aneurysm in the aorta. I quickly flew out to California but found her too heavily sedated to speak with her. I was shocked when the doctor came out to tell the family that Mom's heart had given out during surgery. She was only sixty-two. I have inherited her tan skin coloring from a mixture of East Asian genes (including Chinese, Vietnamese, Indonesian, Thai, Khmer, and Myanmar). More importantly, I now realize she also passed on to me her compassion for peoples of all races.

The Middle East oil embargo in 1973/74 caused an energy crisis in the US. I received many requests for my old research papers on solar energy. By 1977, New Mexico State's Physical Science Laboratory was at the forefront of solar research. I could not pass up the offer from NMSU of a joint appointment as senior research engineer and mechanical engineering professor. It did not take long before I became the director of the New Mexico Solar Energy Institute (NMSEI). Administration (not my forte) and leadership were new challenges requiring new skills. To live what I preached, we built a passive solar house that Monika designed. The move was a culture shock for our children. They were not fully reconciled with their new location until after we made a trip back to Knoxville a year later. Then they realized their new experiences had helped them grow and gain a valuable, wider worldview.

It would take volumes to describe in detail all the different projects and growth that occurred in the three years I headed up the NMSEI. The hardest thing to learn as an administrator was having a thick skin against criticism! Solar energy had become a political game with serious problems. For example, some projects were designed to benefit Native Americans. But they were suspicious of white folks. They felt the low-tech solar facilities were given to them while the rest of the population was enjoying the more convenient fuels.

I still had tenure at the University of Tennessee (UT). We moved back to Knoxville when I accepted the position of director of the Energy, Environment and Resources Center (EERC) at UT. The EERC was working with the Oak Ridge National Laboratory on the BEPS program (Building Energy Performance Standards). Energy consumption and waste would be substantially reduced through new building codes, research on new building materials, and better designs. However, in January 1981, Ronald Reagan became president, supply-side economics took over, and the BEPS program was canceled.

I soon realized that the climate at work had changed. The federal solar tax credits were repealed. I was becoming bored with routine administrative work and began looking for a new venture. I didn't tell Monika when I applied for the engineering dean's job at the University of Michigan-Dearborn and went there for an interview. Then I could hardly believe they actually offered me the position!

The University of Michigan-Dearborn (UM-D) turned out to be a good place for starting as a dean. I could implement my own vision of what I wanted the engineering college to be. For a few months, I was commuting between Tennessee and Michigan, winding up my responsibilities at the EERC while slowly getting involved at UM-D. The vice chancellor gave me time to prepare for my new duties. He even allowed me two months off to serve as visiting professor at a new university in Doha, Qatar. Since the Dearborn area has the highest concentration of Arab people outside the Middle East, this experience was useful for gaining more insight into that culture.

When a flyer arrived in the mail describing a one-week Creativity Institute to be held at the University of Wisconsin-Whitewater, I decided Monika and I should attend. This week radically turned us around in the way we think and use our brain. We were assigned to separate teams, and both of us learned we had been born creative right-brain thinkers. But our "different" ideas had received so much negative responses in school that we buried this ability. Now it was as if a dam broke. But when we taught a pilot workshop on creative problem solving to Ford engineers, the company decided they did not want this training after all. However, our work was not in vain—it was the start of much writing and teaching on this subject for many years. But it also increased my propensity for risk taking.

When the chancellor announced his retirement, I had the support of the UM-D faculty to apply for the position, based on my accomplishments. A search firm was involved in the process, and they hinted that I should withdraw, which I declined to do. After a final interview, I was informed that the regents had chosen the other candidate. Although I put up a good front, I was devastated and felt betrayed.

Monika on the other hand was relieved. The wife of the retiring chancellor had shared with her that one of the requirements of the position was being a good liar—she often had to pretend to be delighted at entertaining people she despised, just because they were prospects who might make a substantial financial contribution to the university. Thus, Monika did not feel this job was what God had in mind for us.

As for me, I had miscalculated the political climate—the regents were under pressure to achieve better gender and racial balance in the top administration of the University of Michigan system, and here was a chance to achieve this with one stroke. Being biracial was not sufficient, neither was what Dr. Bill Spurgeon, the CAD/CAM director at UM-D, said about me: "The dean is a man with a vision—a leader. He had a vision of where the school should go, and he took it there."

Shortly after this, I received a letter from the University of Toledo, inviting me to apply to be dean of engineering. Thus, it came about that I resigned from the University of Michigan-Dearborn and accepted this new challenge. That the new job came with a substantial salary increase didn't hurt, and Monika was happy we would be purchasing a neat little house with a dozen oak trees on the west side of town. Monika and I co-authored the book, *Creative Problem Solving: An Introductory Course for Engineering Students,* and we worked together in developing the Saturday Academy for secondary school students and their parents and teachers. I introduced a six-year faculty development program, and the college moved to a new campus and transitioned to computer use in teaching, with labs for students.

While I was working hard to advance in my career, our children's lives were changed by tragedy: a broken back, a tick bite that led to incurable chronic Lyme disease, a marriage ending due to conflicts related to AIDS, the loss of friends through suicide, murder in Chicago, and an automobile accident caused by an illegal immigrant. We found that God's comfort and the prayers of other Christians sustained them during these devastating circumstances. Blessings then came when they met and married supportive spouses, followed by the birth of their children.

Before I continue, I want to share excerpts of letters my children wrote to me for my fiftieth birthday.

From Arnold:

Dear Dad: Growing up, I can remember envying kids whose parents never punished them. They could do anything, lead an undisciplined life, and get away with it. Looking back now, I'm very thankful for the strong authority figure you were. Instead of catering to what your children wanted, you decided to do what was right, even though both parties didn't really enjoy it! That's one thing I've always admired about you and had a profound effect on my life—you are a man of integrity, who will do the right thing, regardless of what others think. Through your strong leadership, discipline, and love, I have seen God's great love for me.

From Alfred:

Dear Dad: I think the most important thing you taught me was to have the right set of values. I remember growing up how much you stressed the things that really mattered: family, religion, and education Although I didn't always appreciate it then, I can look back now and see how much I benefitted from your priorities. It is particularly remarkable that you are so family-oriented, coming from your background. That's one thing I very much admire about you—you're really self-made. You don't look down on people because of race or social standing; you judge people according to their competence and what they've done with their opportunities.

From Anne:

Dear Daddy: It's really hard for me not to brag about you and Mom. You're so talented and hardworking. You have taught us what is most important in life—God, our family, education, honesty, love, hard work, diligence, even humor. I especially want to express thanks to you for making us kids feel like we're so special to you. I really value all those times you took us out on Sundays to talk with us individually, just by ourselves (and eat French fries). Thank you for taking us traveling as a family all around the US and Europe! I appreciate all the sacrifices you made so that we could have a good education and grow up in a good home.

From Andrew:

Dad: It's funny how my perceptions of life have changed as I've grown and matured. I used to resent the discipline I received. I perceived our family as being somehow different and therefore inferior to those around us. Now I can see the worth of the discipline; I can see the vanity of trying to be "normal," and I can see the positive influences our being different has had on my life.

You will always be a source of inspiration and strength to me. Your fidelity and solidity are rare qualities these days. Now I know how unusual it is to have a father like you. You were always there, faithful and strong, loving and giving, sacrificing yourself in so many ways to provide for your family. What I especially appreciate are the spiritual advantages. Having a Christian father, a Christian family, is a rarity these days. I thank you for providing such a nurturing environment while I was growing up, that I was able to come into my own knowledge of Jesus Christ as Lord and Savior. Your effect on my life is truly eternal. Now, as I contemplate taking a wife and starting my own family, I can only pray that I will be as good a husband and father as you have been. I love you.

I won't say much more about our children, their very much-admired spouses, and the fourteen unique grandchildren that have been born to them—they have their own stories to tell. But I want to say a few words about how my career changes have affected Monika.

When we moved from Brookings to Knoxville, Monika grieved the loss of her church friends. Almost immediately, she and the children became painfully acquainted with poison ivy when clearing vines on our property to plant a blueberry patch. A highpoint for her was hearing Corrie Ten Boom, the well-known survivor of a German concentration camp, speak at the University of Tennessee. She was over 80, and her energetic message about forgiveness simply astonished us. Monika joined a women's group at Cedar Springs Presbyterian Church, helping to roll bandages for missions and doing other work projects. She suggested a brief devotional and prayer should be included, which was happily adopted.

So that Monika could design us a passive solar house in Las Cruces, I taught her basic heat transfer principles and how to do heat gain and loss calculations. In the midst of the construction, her father called to say that her mother was terminally ill with colon cancer. She could hear the tears in his voice. A week after Monika reached Switzerland, her mother died peacefully. Her father and the two daughters had been able to say good-bye before she fell into a coma. She was 70. We were thankful she did not have to suffer long.

Monika and I gave public tours of our solar house. The US Department of Energy and the US Department of Housing and Urban Development had a national design competition for passive solar houses, and she submitted a generic design which won a national award. She used the prize money to start her own consulting business. One of her projects funded by the State of New Mexico was to develop a simple design manual for passive solar homes adapted to the different climatic regions in the state.

My superior, one of the vice-presidents at NMSU, was also Monika's boss. When the design manual (including sample blueprints) was completed, he sat on it for weeks and would not release it for publication, even though many people begged to get copies, so they could build their own solar homes. She finally wrote to the governor to complain about the delay. The vice-president was irate at me for not "controlling" my wife. I had to tell him that she was her own competent and independent person and not a staff member of the

NMSEI. This constituted Monika's contribution to solar energy as well as to the cultural change in women's rights in the 1970s!

Monika fondly recalls the evening Bible study we attended with several couples from our church. This was the only time we attended such a study, and she says she still misses it. It helped us to talk about spiritual matters and to pray together.

Then back in Knoxville, Monika designed and built us a two-story passive solar house. TVA bought her plans for their *Solar Homes Portfolio*. Many family members came to visit us during the summer of 1982, to see the World's Fair with the theme, "Energy Turns the World."

I don't think we understood how her stress level was mounting during the years of my career advances and moves. She remembers it this way: *"All this stress resulted in my having a terrible attitude. I felt guilty for having pushed the construction of the Knoxville house. Later, as a dean's spouse and hostess, I felt awkward—I saw myself no longer as a supportive helper but as a hindrance to Edward's career. Simply put, I had no social skills. I was uncomfortable when attending official dinners. The worst situation was when a state senator was telling an awful off-color story, and I asked him to please stop. With the moves, I lost my support system of close Christian friends. I felt isolated and less able to share my feelings with Edward. The cultural gap was widening between us."*

The fifth year at the University of Toledo turned out to be one of the worst periods in my life. I was oblivious that my assistant was an inveterate gossip stirring up trouble. I had brought two graduate students from Dearborn. All my previous graduate students had been male, but now I was mentoring an outstanding female doctoral student. Sadly, we became the target of—I can't describe it in any other way—evil people.

To relieve the almost unbearable stress at Toledo, I began to frequent casinos in Windsor, Canada. Unfortunately, this increasingly became a strong addiction, because I enjoyed the risk taking and wagering ever larger amounts. I hid this activity from Monika, which of course put our marriage in jeopardy and added stress to both of us, once she discovered the truth.

Monika recently heard a testimony of a man who came to Christ, once he realized God meant life to be difficult, because it will draw us to Him. We did learn this lesson, although it was to take a long time.

Monika: Struggles and Blessings Affecting My Faith (1993-2020)

From the time Edward started as dean of engineering at Michigan Technological University in Houghton, the changes in our lives accelerated. After two years, we moved to Ann Arbor for two years, then back to Michigan for two years, followed by a half-year sabbatical in England, with five more years back in our sunny house in Michigan. After we sold it, our solar house in Knoxville became our base, with us living intermittently in eight different places related to Edward's work and providentially provided by God, until we decided to sell our house and move to our current apartment without stairs.

I loved living in the Upper Peninsula of Michigan—until the snow got to be too much. One February, I was utterly transfixed when seeing my first aurora borealis. Wavy curtains of light covered the entire sky, with bright laser beams periodically shooting upward. I loved hiking along Lake Superior beaches, searching for agates and other semi-precious stones to polish. Edward had bought me an old jeep so I could reach the more isolated places of what was locally known as God's country.

Edward and I published several books and papers on creative problem solving. One paper, "Thinking Preferences of Engineering Students: Implication for Curriculum Restructuring," published in the *Journal of Engineering Education* in April 1995, received quite a bit of attention. This is the only paper that listed me as the primary author, since it focused on my research in a six-year longitudinal study.

The decade between 1990 and 2000 was a turning point in engineering education, in that both teaching and learning with computers as well as creativity and teamwork began to be introduced and emphasized. Edward received the Xerox/ASEE Chester Carlson Award in 1994 for innovation in engineering education. This affirmation lifted his spirit for a time.

While in the UK, one weekend stands out especially, when Edward and I went to Lincoln to see the cathedral and adjoining castle, which had a fascinating exhibit on the magna carta and its relationship to the US constitution. Amazing! On the other hand, we were startled when we realized that the congregation in the cathedral consisted mainly of elderly women.

Edward and a British professor teamed up to teach one-week courses for MBS students in Malaysia in July twice and in Singapore every November for nine years, with me doing the thinking styles assessments for these students. Eventually, Ford Motor Company gave me a title, *Management Consultant for Corporate Behavior.* I conducted workshops in industry and universities for faculty, staff, and countless students, sometimes solo and sometimes teaming with Edward (including in Taiwan and South Africa). I also gave talks to Christian women groups.

During these years, sad events were the deaths of Edward's brothers Robert and Chuck, his cousin David, and my sister Lili in Switzerland. Shortly before Lili died of cancer at 60, she shared with me that she had turned to Jesus and was at peace, looking forward to heaven. I thanked God in my heart that she was now safe for all eternity.

After my friend Louise and I cleared Lili's apartment in Switzerland—which took an entire month—I flew to England to join Edward who was at a retreat in Dovedale with Nottingham University staff. The UK customs official asked what my purpose was for coming to England. "I want to go hiking in Dovedale. Can you tell me how to get there?" He gave me several tips and then said: "Give my love to Dovedale." The week there was like balm for my soul; it was like walking in the twenty-third psalm among the sheep-dotted hills and along the smoothly flowing River Dove.

Lili's death is amazingly connected to how God provided the property where a new sanctuary was to be built for Houghton Baptist Church. We had only limited sanctuary and parking lot space. By the time I left for Switzerland when my sister was dying, a suitable and affordable acreage had not yet been identified.

When I returned a month later and attended church the next day, a vote on a proposed site was called. I stood up and asked to be allowed to say a few words: *"I want to remind you that we had agreed to only proceed if enough money was available—that's how we would know God's will. My sister has just died and left me her life insurance in her will. She found the Lord as Savior just weeks earlier and felt sad that she had never tithed. I promised I would tithe both her share and mine on this insurance, and the amount, when converted to dollars, will be about $20,000."*

Our pastor's wife told me later that he was so astonished, he could have been blown over with a feather. He woke up that morning with a heavy heart, knowing that the money on hand was only half of what was needed to buy this particular hill-top land. Isn't the Lord's timing marvelous? I'm sure Lili is rejoicing in heaven. Then I could hardly believe God gave me the wisdom and responsibility to make unilateral decisions during the sanctuary's construction. Once the building was done and we moved away, I no longer had (or needed) the special gift of leadership.

Here I want to share the most surprising and miraculous experience of my life. One day when I was walking downstairs, carrying a sleeping grandchild on my right arm, I tripped three or four steps up from the wooden vestibule. In an instant mental time-lapse I saw myself falling on top of the baby, crushing her in the process. Instead, I felt someone catching me from behind and laying me down carefully by the front door. The baby did not even wake up. My ankle was swelling and painful, so I did not move. When my daughter-in-law returned from shopping, she asked, "What are you doing on the floor?" I knew, the child had a guardian angel, but I took this as a sign that I was protected as well!

After my surgery for breast cancer and the four years of treatment with Arimidex and Femara, I have been a member of a cancer support group in our church. I told my story of how God gave me comfort and strength during these years through His Word on particular topics, such as sin and forgiveness *(1 John 1:9);* God's will and God's way (*Romans 12:1-2, James 1:2-5);* God's purpose and our attitude *(Philippians 2:3-5,13-15);* and God's tool for fighting spiritual battles provided through His armor *(Ephesians 6:10-18).* Several members of the group have gone on to be with our Lord. Supporting each other and the families through prayer has been a ministry and blessing.

Starting in 2016, we have attended a three-day senior celebration each year at the Billy Graham Training Center at The Cove near Asheville, North Carolina, even during the pandemic. We have been deeply blessed and strengthened by the encouraging messages of God's love for us. The topics were:

- God's Purpose for Our Lives from Ephesians, *Chapter 1:1-14.*
- Caleb, Barnabas, David, and Philip: Be a witness to what Jesus has done for us.
- *Psalms 1, 2, 103, 116, 139:* Meet Jesus in "the deep place where nobody goes" as told by Jill Briscoe.

- Receive a Blessing and Be a Blessing *(Numbers 6:22-27, Psalm 1, Genesis 12:1-3, Ephesians 4:29).*
- Encounters with Jesus, Then and Now *(Luke 8: 26-39, John 8:2-11, John 1:35-51, Matthew 5:38-48).* Questions to think about were: Do people see the heart of God in you? Are you fighting evil with good? Are you doing the unexpected by extending forgiveness? Are you walking the second mile?
- The Uncomfortable Will of God: Trusting His Plan and Resting in His Power *(the Book of Jonah).* God's grace is in the storms He sends. He patiently pursues us.

Edward: Gambling Addiction and Slide into the Pit

In Toledo, I filed a lawsuit for defamation of character jointly with my graduate student. Two department heads and Monika strongly advised against it, because in their view no real damage had been done to my marriage, my salary, or my position at the university.

In addition to mounting lawyer's fees, the case began to take a toll in stress and time required to answer insulting or merely stupid discovery documents. After I spent thousands of dollars, the university was able to transfer the case to Columbus, where it now had all the resources of the State of Ohio available. My lawyer said this would triple the costs, and he did not think the case was winnable in Columbus. I had no choice but to withdraw, even though I felt badly about the injustice which now had no legal remedy, neither f or me nor my student.

Although the excitement of casino slot machines or blackjack temporarily provided stress relief and distracted me from anger and bitterness, my spiritual slide began to accelerate. I forgot the fine Christians I had encountered in my life. I distanced myself emotionally, even from Monika; I did not want to hear about forgiveness, although she loyally stood by me through all false accusations.

Unexpectedly I was invited for an interview to be dean of engineering at Michigan Technological University (MTU). I was candid with the provost (who would be my immediate supervisor) about the trouble stirred up against me by a few evil people in Toledo. He assured me this made no difference—he would not tolerate any gossip at Michigan Tech.

I gladly accepted this better job at a prestigious engineering college, twice the size of Toledo's. The mechanical engineering department where I would be tenured was one of the largest in the nation. Although my appointment in Toledo had just been renewed, it was a relief to leave. Sadly, before long, the malicious gossip from Toledo reached Michigan Tech. It proved difficult to head up the college because of continual whispers.

Therefore, barely two years as dean of engineering there, I wanted to return to teaching as a faculty member, hoping this would reduce stress. When Russ Smith, for whom I had done consulting work at Ford Motor Company, heard that I had stepped down as dean, he immediately called, "Can you come to Ford to help me develop the new C3P program for high-tech education and training in CAD/CAM/CAE/PIM?" I had all of two weeks to move!

Let me explain these acronyms. They stand for computer-aided design, computer-aided manufacturing, computer-aided engineering and product information management. I found out that C3P was the largest computer-based technology effort in Ford's history.

I enjoyed being at Ford. The C3P program grew rapidly, and several times we had to move to larger quarters. Although I managed to do my work at Ford well (as a "functioning addict"), casino gambling in Windsor now became all-consuming, and my marriage and future financial security came into grave jeopardy. I was headed to the bottom of the pit and had to face the truth: gambling was in control of me.

Pathological gamblers have an incredible talent for self-deception which prevents them from recognizing the traits, dangers, and progression of addiction—they either deny they have a problem, refuse to talk about it, or believe they can control or overcome it in their own power.

When gamblers deceive others in attempts to hide the gambling activity, they are on a slippery downward slope, leading to loss of integrity. One in five pathological gamblers will attempt suicide (I was one of them). These gamblers are typically highly intelligent, competitive, and well-educated; they enjoy challenges and risk. They are often workaholics and have problems with impulse control.

Casinos (and/or lotteries) are permitted in all states except Hawaii and Utah. In addition, there are thousands of websites for all types of gambling. According to ESPN, by 2018, all states except Utah, Idaho and Wisconsin have legalized betting on sports. So-called gaming is big business with aggressive marketing to get people from all walks of life hooked by exploiting human weakness and greed. Casinos always win! Space in casinos is allocated to maximize the activities that make the most money for the casinos. When no seats are available for table games, players will gravitate toward the slots. Casinos gain 75% or more of their total income from the slot machines (which are highly addictive).

According to Gamblers Anonymous, gambling addiction is a progressive and incurable disease. It can be arrested if there is a strong desire *not* to gamble and if the gambler is motivated to get better through complete abstinence! Sadly, we did not recognize the true extent of my gambling addiction for a long time.

The following list of psychological mind tricks describes the process that makes it so tough to admit gambling addiction and why recovery is so difficult. It is summarized from Chapter 3, *Addiction & Grace* by Gerald G. May, M.D.

Psychological Mind Tricks Involved in Self-Deception

1. *Denial:* Not recognizing a problem exists and also not wanting to think about it.
2. *Repression:* To keep from recognizing the truth, quiet times, prayer and meditation are avoided. Instead, noisy TV or music cover up a fear of boredom.
3. *Rationalization*: When denial and repression fail, excuses are the next defense to justify and reinforce the addictive behavior.
4. *Hiding and Pretense:* When the truth can no longer be hidden from the addict, it becomes increasingly important to hide it from others through lies, pretense, and isolation. Depression, guilt, and loss of integrity are covered up.
5. *Procrastination:* The more creative and intelligent the person, the more inventive and complex will be the plans to quit, so that action will be repeatedly delayed.

6. *I Can Handle It:* When a person succeeds in stopping the addictive behavior for a while, the most devious mind trick of all appears. Pride sets the stage for sabotage and thinking, "I can do the behavior without becoming enslaved again," or "I can do it in moderation."
7. *Breakdown:* The fall from pride is heart-breaking. Suicide is considered. Fortunately, not all addictions progress to this devastating point, but the mind tricks will continue, unless a spiritual transformation occurs.

By August 1999, I finally admitted I had become a pathological gambler. I prayed for help and wrote down three goals: (1) stop gambling, (2) prepare for retirement, and (3) renew marriage vows. To prepare for retirement, I annuitized the funds left in my university retirement accounts. That money would now be available to Monika in case something happened to me. She is convinced this was God providing for her.

To improve our relationship and to let her know I loved her, I proposed that we should have a service in our church to renew our wedding vows on our fortieth anniversary. In a way I was surprised Monika had not left me years ago. She says she had been tempted while we lived in Ann Arbor but had learned from the Bible that this would not be right.

A few days later, I suffered a severe gallstone attack. When I saw my doctor, she scheduled laparoscopic surgery for the following morning. I ended up in intensive care for two days. The largest gallstone had been as big as an egg. Also, I was diagnosed with diabetes and high blood pressure. These sudden health problems jolted me into rethinking my life. Alas, as soon as I felt better, I stopped praying and abandoned my goal to stop gambling.

During the fall of 1999 I became eligible for a sabbatical. I was appointed special professor of business to work in the emerging Institute for Enterprise and Innovation (UNIEI) at Nottingham University. I felt highly honored by this position in one of the most prestigious universities in England. It allowed me to take a week off each month, which made it possible to continue consulting with Ford (and continue to gamble in Windsor). The main benefit of my involvement with the UNIEI was that I began teaching and writing books in the area of creativity, entrepreneurship, and innovation.

The summer after I returned to Michigan Tech from England, I continued my consulting work for Ford Motor Company. As my savings evaporated in the casino, my self-respect and caring for others deteriorated even more. The quality of my teaching began to suffer. I lost the concern I had held for decades—that my students learn. And I also stopped doing research.

I was not taking my depression seriously nor realized the direct relationship to gambling. The more I gambled, the more the losses mounted and the more depressed I became. I vacillated between hope that things would get better with the next win and remorse as I kept losing. I felt condemned and disconnected from my family. The energy needed to play with my grandchildren when visiting them was almost more than I could muster—I just went through the motions.

Monika was finally able to let go of her attempts to change me—she was leaving me in God's hands and trusted Him to deal with me. But this spiritual change made me feel there was an insurmountable gulf between us that did not allow any intimacy. Her prayers would eventually be answered, in God's perfect timing. But I had many lessons to learn until then. But right now, I had lost all hope that God would help me; I felt I did not deserve His help.

More deeply in the grip of gambling addiction, I began to realize by 2003 that neither satisfaction in my daily work, having a successful professional career, nor keeping the respect of my children, the innocent trust of my grandchildren, or the love of my wife kept me from tumbling ever faster into a black abyss of despair. The American Dream had turned to dust.

After another dreary night of heavy losses with loans I could not repay, yet unable to sleep, I gazed at the array of pill bottles with my medications set out on the nightstand. Here was a way out from all my troubles and pain! Without another thought, I gulped down the entire supply. Then the shock and stupidity of what I had done cleared my mind long enough to call the hotel's front desk for help to get me to the nearest hospital.

I have not met a single person that says gambling satisfies. Gamblers are betting their lives and losing—it creates a hole in the soul. I hardly remember when I was taken to the hospital by ambulance and had my stomach pumped after swallowing the pills in my despondency. It was an unpleasant and expensive experience.

Some people are instantly and miraculously delivered from addiction. I believe my road to recovery is more typical, in that it has involved serious battles and drawn-out struggle to escape from the pit. To help others, I feel I must share what I learned.

Edward: Spiritual Awakening and Sabotage

As special professor of business for the University of Nottingham, I was flying to Kuala Lumpur in November 2001 to attend a meeting, before proceeding to Singapore to teach. The flight from Detroit to Osaka was fourteen hours and from Osaka to Kuala Lumpur seven hours, and I looked forward to some rest and relaxation on this long trip. Shortly after takeoff from Detroit, the refrain from a hymn, "It is well with my soul," kept going through my head. But as I eased back in my seat to sleep, the hymn's wording changed to "Is it well with your soul?" I could not sleep for most of the trip. This question forced me to examine how my spiritual life slid as I became increasingly ensnared in gambling. I could no longer take comfort in my belief that gambling was okay—the lines were becoming very clear: gambling was stealing.

It was late in 2001 when Monika began attending a Bible study in our church for people with addictions. She went alone—I was not ready to admit to others I had a problem. Monika hoped to learn if there was anything she could do to help me. She found that SAFE (Setting Addicts Free Eternally) was designed to aid anyone to become more stable emotionally through studying and memorizing the Word of God, whether addicted or not.

Key principles of the SAFE program's "Journey to Freedom" were:

- Christ is the only secure foundation for our life and the long-term answer to addictions.
- Saturating the mind with specific verses from God's Word is the only way to recondition the subconscious mind, thereby changing old behavior patterns through a hundred repetitions in a day if necessary!
- Our goal must parallel God's perfect will for our lives. We can have a healthy mind and learn to control our emotions when conformity to God's principles and purpose. Also, the Bible strongly condemns greed as idolatry, an especially odious sin in God's eyes.

After repeating the seventeen-week cycle three times, Monika became a leader in this small-group study. She learned to trust and claim God's promises in the Bible. This broke the emotional co-dependence on my impulsive behavior and she no longer feared the future (see Appendix 3).

By late 2002, I began to seek help. I tentatively started attending SAFE meetings. I mostly sat in the back and listened to what the others were sharing; I did not take time to do the daily homework assignments nor memorize the weekly Bible verse. When in the Detroit area, I went to Gamblers Anonymous meetings. Since one of the requirements was to stay away from all gambling, I signed out of Casino Windsor. I was now barred from the gaming area of Ontario casinos and could be arrested and charged for trespass if I gambled.

I found my efforts were much more difficult than I had ever imagined. How was I to fight a lifetime penchant for an activity that I had considered not to be illegal, immoral, or unethical? Although I marked 2003 as the year to pay off my debts and stop gambling, it was my worst year in terms of losses. I was staying away from Windsor Casino. But when I happened to drive by the brand-new MotorCity Casino in Detroit one day in early March, I was curious to find out what it was like on the inside. This was enough to get me started there, and I began to spend a lot of time playing video poker for the most part.

In July 2003, I stood in front of the entire congregation of Houghton Baptist Church to tell my story, admit my gambling addiction, and ask for prayer. Up to the final moment before reaching the pulpit, I was not sure if I wanted to go through with it. A battle was going on in my mind. What would people think of me? Monika encouraged me and promised that I would be surprised at what would happen.

She was right—I was touched when several people came up to me afterwards and with tears in their eyes shared that they, too, were struggling with the temptation to gamble. I did not realize it at the time, but now I believe this testimony was the most important step in my recovery, even though it seemed to launch an all-out attack by the forces of hell upon my resolve—I cannot remember any time when I was more in the grip of addiction than in the following months.

Then in March 2008 I had to confess to Monika that I was in the throes of a serious relapse in my road to recovery. I did not expect this to happen, although I had been warned. I was not vigilant, and "pride comes before the fall." After almost three years of staying away from casinos, I had decided around mid-March 2007 that it would be safe for me to go and check out the new MGM Casino in Detroit. At first, I tried to limit my gambling to modest amounts, but it didn't take long to get me hooked again, especially on the slot machines. By mid-fall, I switched from the MGM to gamble exclusively at the Greektown Casino.

I truly wanted 2009 to be the year of a new beginning for my life. As a first step, I handed Monika a stack about eight inches high of the W-2G vouchers of my gambling winnings which she needed for the income tax returns. Again, I was appalled at the tax consequences of my gambling. This finally forced me to pay attention to the last lesson in the SAFE program in order to understand what was happening to me.

I discovered that my situation was far from unique—rather, the phenomenon of ***sabotage*** was a common problem on the path to recovery from addiction. The questions I needed to answer were, "Why did I sabotage my life when I was doing well? What made me return to the old pattern of behavior? Was it a poor self-image, pride, or resistance to change?"

Pride was easy to recognize. As a self-made man, I felt entitled to use my hard-earned money my way. But I failed to be a good steward, and as a minimum, to pay a tithe. I felt I had provided adequately for Monika by giving her the annuities to run our household. I was oblivious to Tennessee law that prescribes an equitable distribution of a couple's assets. Truly, I had robbed both God and Monika of their shares by my selfish viewpoint. Even though I acknowledged the guiding hand of God behind the scenes, I still felt that it was I who made all the decisions and did the hard work to educate myself and to advance in my career. I felt I could control the gambling.

Monika: Recovery and Never-Ending Love

During the dark winter of 2009/10, I slid into a deep depression. This was more than the usual seasonal syndrome; I had a complete burnout. I had finished a careful revision of the entrepreneurship book and was exhausted. I was on high blood pressure medication and could barely function. I had to stop helping Edward with his class materials or pinch-hit teaching the design classes when he was out of town.

Then Edward announced that he had accepted a one-year appointment as distinguished visiting professor at the US Air Force Academy in Colorado Springs. That felt like an additional blow to me. My friend Tisha who was familiar with that area of the Rocky Mountains tried to cheer me up by saying, "You will love it there." This turned out to be the case indeed.

In Colorado Springs, we attended Village Seven Presbyterian Church. They offered a class on Wednesday evenings—the Dave Ramsey Financial Peace University. What we learned about budgeting is still helping us in our retirement.

In addition, the church had many outreach programs. I began attending a *Celebrate Recovery* group. Although the program was mainly designed for people with addictions, it helped me with my co-dependency. I could grieve the losses and hurts caused by Edward's gambling and then extend forgiveness. However, this was not a one-time event but had to be repeated along the ups and downs of his recovery. But I can say that it truly was the start of an ongoing healing process. Just being in the group with other ladies and supporting each other through prayer was consoling, though difficult to describe. Because I came to rely on prayer more and more, one dear Bible teacher called me a warrior princess. I have never told her how much comfort this provided to me as I struggled to build a healthier self-image—not focused on my failings, but on how God saw me. The faith He has given me has been crucial in my own recovery.

Soon after we were back in Michigan in the fall of 2011, I was diagnosed with age-related wet macular degeneration in both eyes, an incurable condition inherited from my father. Injections of Lucentis (an expensive cancer drug that can shrink capillaries that leak in the retina) have kept my vision steady at 20/30, which my doctor thinks is quite extraordinary—but which I ultimately attribute to God's mercy and many prayers by family and friends.

Edward still finds it painful to talk about his slow recovery, so I will continue the story. Sabotage kept rearing its ugly head. Now the excuse had changed to, "I'm just doing it for recreation and fun, like most people at the casino." Or, like one blind pastor whom we consulted recommended, "Why don't you join him, Monika?" I did go with Edward once, but the atmosphere there felt evil and oppressive. He eventually found me outside, weeping among trees covered with snow.

By 2014, Edward was determined to make a fresh start and stop gambling. He still wanted to do it his own way, but he promised me he would let me know if he relapsed—then he would seek counseling and therapy. He had run up against a boundary—no more funds that he could use. He was resolved not to go into debt again.

He kept his promise, and we went to see a counselor at our church. It took one session to accept that, "All of us are sinners who need a savior and redeemer." He continued, "Edward, you are a son of the King, an ambassador, a priest of God, a pilgrim on the way to heaven, a servant, yet a brother, friend and heir of Christ!" Wow! What a precious, healing difference to being seen and called a rotten gambler!

Now Edward was ready to write a letter from his heart to his grandchildren about what he had to learn the hard way.

My dear Grandchildren: These steps about my struggles to recovery are above all warnings not just for you, but to myself as well!

1. *First of all, if you are not a gambler, don't start. If you are a teenager, you are three times more likely to become a pathological gambler than an adult. If you are an occasional player, quit before it is too late. This goes for casinos as well as on-line gambling (or merely playing the lottery or sports betting or having fun with friends playing poker). Don't take this risk!*

2. *If you at any time have become a compulsive gambler, there are important things you can do. The first is to acknowledge that you are addicted and cannot help yourself. You must be motivated to want to change!*

3. *Next comes forgiveness. I had to accept God's forgiveness for my wrong actions, for wasting time and resources in gambling and hurting my family. I had to stop making excuses. But the key was to forgive the people towards whom he felt bitter. It took a long time to overcome my anger. Forgiving was not a one-time event but had to be repeated over and over again. Finally, I also had to forgive myself, and I had to humbly accept Monika's forgiveness.*

4. *Do everything you can to grow in your spiritual life and strengthen your personal relationship with Jesus Christ, God's Son. Be consistent in daily reading God's Word and praying, giving thanks! Then obey the directions God wants you to take or to patiently wait for Him to show you. Carry out His purpose for your life! Be accountable to a spiritually mature person. Advice from a counselor was a crucial stepping stone in my recovery, as was writing this book.*

5. *Improve your communication skills and be more open with your close family members,*

especially if you tend to "shield" from confrontation or discussing subjects that are uncomfortable or painful. As a recovering gambler, stop "playing behind the vest."

6. *Learn to handle emotional stress. What is most important in your life? Reframe negative experiences, so they can become a source of blessing. Learn to value yourself. Seek treatment for depression. Inform your primary physician of your addiction—he or she may be able to point you to resources and can approve insurance payments for counseling. At the least, the doctor will not prescribe Mirapex as a treatment, since this drug can cause compulsive gambling as a side effect.*

7. *Set new priorities for your life—things that will give your life new meaning. Develop self-discipline. Watch out for greed; instead, practice good stewardship and focus on what you can do for others. I'm still working on this! I want to be able to look you in the eye and say, "I used to gamble, but I don't do that anymore." I know I am upward bound in the Kingdom of God; to Him be the glory!*

With my love and humble prayers, Your Yehyeh

To fight his strong gambling addiction, Edward did something I believe made a big difference to turn him towards God. On long drives across the Upper Peninsula, he would play the harmonica while listening to hymns on a CD. One time, he was stopped by a state trooper who was warning drivers of icy road conditions ahead. "Do you play while driving?" he asked when he saw the open box of harmonicas on the passenger seat. Before answering, Edward needed to know, "Is it against the law?" "No, certainly not," he chuckled. Then Edward explained, "I often play to keep alert while driving." But the hymns did more than that—they drew him closer to God. Even now, he listens to instrumental hymns to help him sleep at night. And earlier in the evening, he plays a soothing lullaby or favorite hymns for me.

In our retirement years, we have found contentment that is deepening our companionship and love for each other. We are respecting our differences with joy. For example, when I am out on a wildflower excursion with my friend, Tisha, I am glad that Edward can treat himself to a shrimp meal. We do appreciate being at the same stage in coping with vision, hearing, walking and memory problems. Because of the encircling incredible love of God, our love will never end. We know for certain:

Love is patient, love is kind. It does not envy, it does not boast, it is not proud. It does not dishonor others, it is not self-seeking, it is not easily angered; it keeps no record of wrongs. Love does not delight

in evil but rejoices with the truth. It always protects, always trusts, always hopes, always perseveres (1 Corinthians 13:4-7).

Years ago, we attended a seminar on Gary Chapman's *Five Love Languages* in an effort to communicate better. To my surprise, I discovered that I may be suffering from attention deficit disorder. Edward had noticed that I was easily distracted by visual clues around me, when he tried to talk to me. But our lives were busy, and our communication skills did not improve.

Now we find we are subconsciously using each other's love languages. Edward is doing the kitchen cleanup each evening, and I appreciate this as a sacrificial act of service. I on the other hand am rubbing Edward's feet while we are sitting on our sofa watching TV after dinner. Also, I tenderly "tuck him in" when he goes to bed. Both activities involve physical touch. Gift-giving and verbal affirmation are strictly secondary between us (but are nice when given to us by others). Because of our severe dissonance in diurnal rhythms, the best time to share quality time is during early afternoons.

I read in the book *Sacred Marriage* that just because difficulties arise between husband and wife, this does not mean the couple isn't meant to be together for life. Marriage is not primarily for making us happy but for making us holy! It has been a comfort to hear this and to realize that we are still a work in progress.

When Edward was in Shanghai in August 2016, he wrote me a love letter from the place where his story began. The letter is special, because writing about his feelings is hard for him.

My Dear Sweetheart:
As I am sitting here in a Holiday Inn room, I am thinking back to August of 1952, when I left a very different Shanghai as a frightened, scrawny and lost fourteen-year-old.

I can't help but think of Father Peter. I know now that he was doing God's work by helping me leave Shanghai on a path to meet you, resulting in our long and loving relationship of more than half a century. I have been blessed far beyond of what I deserve, with you as my caring and loving wife and helper, and with four incredible children. Our children's faith in God is largely due to your example.

In working with you on our book and recounting the years of happiness and challenges we faced, God has been merciful, faithful and patient with me, especially in adversity. I thank God for you, our children with their own wonderful spouses, and our precious grandchildren. For the remaining years of my life, I pray that He will give me the strength to be less selfish and more considerate and loving towards you.

I will try to be more sensitive to your needs and feelings. I want to take good care of you, as you have taken care of me since we married. I still feel that you are my sunshine, like during our courtship days, and I'm glad that we still feel the same way about each other. It is difficult for me to find words to express my deep love for you. My love for you is eternal.

Forever yours, Edward

Now all that remains to be told is how we made it through 2020, the year of the Covid-19 pandemic.

As a love gift, Edward had planned to take me on a train trip through the Canadian Rockies, but flights were cancelled and the border was closed. I still appreciate the thought, although I doubt that we would be physically able do it in the future.

In early 2020, I fell three times, the third time breaking my right femur. An ambulance took me to the hospital (after I was given fentanyl for the pain). In emergency, after an x-ray, I was scheduled for hip replacement surgery the next day. No fentanyl in the hospital! The surgery turned out to be around 5 in the afternoon, as several other patients were in line for this specialist. The whole day is hazy in my memory. When a very young-looking fellow wearing scrubs came to see me the next morning, I asked: "Who are you?" He was the doctor who had done the surgery—I did not recall that he had explained to me the day before how the hip replacement would be done.

Then the lockdown due to the pandemic started while I was in rehab and physical therapy. During early autumn, until Spring 2021, I became increasingly depressed, due to the isolation and the results of the election. On top of this, my computer broke and took weeks for repairs. But we were thankful to be able to get the Pfizer Covid-19 vaccination in February.

But where was God during the worst depression? After dark, rainy days and in emotional pain from family division, I was crying in the night and couldn't sleep. I started to pray "in the deep place where nobody goes"—a special place where my soul could go to meet with Jesus who was there waiting for me. This is like a sunny garden, with slabs of rock to sit on. I sat down next to Jesus, and He put His arm around me in a tender hug. I experienced such consolation and peace—truly the gift of the Holy Spirit as the Comforter.

Then I looked up into Christ's face. I am utterly incapable in trying to describe the love in His face and eyes that were looking at me. I knew of course from the Bible that God loved me, but to actually see it close up, the immensity of it! He had been rejected, betrayed, was beaten, lied about, and then suffered torture and an excruciating death because of my sins, and yet He loved me, even me, especially me in that moment. He keeps forgiving my sins, extends undeserved mercy, and gives me His righteousness. Now I want to follow Him more faithfully, with all my heart, soul, mind and strength, until He calls me home. And I very much thank Him for Edward and that we are still together.

The cultural change that is disturbing to our family is the discrimination against people with Asian features that is rearing its ugly and irrational head.

Also, what is particularly troubling is an almost wholesale departure of moral judgment from politics and public life. There is an absence of critical thinking skills that would allow people to properly and rationally evaluate what they hear in the news or on social media. Both Edward and I love America and its "flag full of stars." We are very concerned about the attacks on Christian values, on which the Constitution is founded and the general lack of knowledge among our young people about our country's history and how we can preserve our freedoms. There is a spiritual war going on, and it is becoming more overt and affecting our family and friends Are we under God's judgment for having turned away from Him?

But the only issue with eternal consequences is the right to life. Where are over 60 million babies in the US, a large portion of them African American? Are we still complicit in more murders? Why do black lives matter, but not black unborn lives? We do not want our tax dollars used to pay for abortions. The Hyde amendment needs to be renewed for 2022.

Here is the link to the video that Mark Reda (a Christian musician) created from a meditation slideshow with photos my friend Tisha and I took in the spring of 2019. It came out on January 5, 2021. Praise God! Talk about His perfect timing!

https://youtu.be/VZvbrlbNdQ8

Edward recently handed me a song he wants to have at his memorial service: *"Lord, Im Coming Home"* (W.J. Kirkpatrick, 1892), based on Luke 15:18. It is his final testimony and deeply touches my heart:

I've wandered far away from God, Now I'm coming home; The paths of sin too long I've trod, Lord, I'm coming home.

I've wasted many precious years, I now repent with bitter tears. I'm tired of sin and straying, Lord, I'll trust Thy love, believe Thy word.

My soul is sick, my heart is sore, My stregth renew, my home restore, My only hope, my only plea That Jesus died, and died for me.

I need His cleansing blood I know, Now I'm coming home; Oh, wash me whiter than the snow, Lord, I'm coming home.

Coming home, coming home, never more to roam; Open wide Thine arms of love, Lord, I'm coming home.

In closing, I want to share one more glimpse of God's perfect timing. I recently received a brief email that claimed Edward was gambling again. I instantly knew this was a false assumption. He had been home with me during the entire period of the lockdown. But what was most amazing was that I realized we were free! We passed the test! I experienced complete peace and trust in God having answered our prayers for emotional healing. He provided the perfect ending to our story just at a time when a publisher expressed interest in our book.

Appendix 3 shows that the one plank in the Bridge of Faith that I had questioned for years had been God's timing. Now He confirmed that I could completely trust this attribute of His character! Now we praise Him and pray that our story of redemption will be an encouragement for many to turn to God for salvation and eternal life.

The Lord is our rock, our fortress and our deliverer;
He is our shield, our refuge, and our stronghold
(adapted from Psalm 18:1-2).

Lord Jesus, thank you for your awesome, never-ending love! You said,

Peace be with you!
As the Father has sent me, I am sending you
(John 20:21).

Appendix 1

Lumsdaine Family Tree

This information is excerpted from *An Australian Family (1997)* by Geoffrey Lumsdaine, ISBN 0-646 31177-8. Part 1 gives examples of some notable ancestors; Part 2 summarizes the descendants of Captain William Lumsdaine of Scotland.

Part 1: Some Notable Family Ancestors

Tracing ancestors in a direct line can be extremely difficult, but when a connection to a royal family is found, it is much easier to follow a path which is well documented by historians and genealogists over the centuries.

In 1739, James Lumsdaine of Rennyhill married Mary Lillias Sharp. Her mother was a Drummond and a great-great-great-great-great-granddaughter of King James VI of Scotland. She is the grandmother of William Lumsdaine (1792-1830)—see Part 2.

There is an unbroken line of descent from Alpin King of Scotland, Egbert King of the English, Alfred the Great King of England (849-899), Rollo Chief of the Normans, and Eochaid the Venomous Chief of the Picts circa 780, as well as William the Conqueror, to Mary Lillias and consequently to Clifford Vere Lumsdaine, the father of Edward Lumsdaine.

Part 2: Descendants of Captain William Lumsdaine

The generations are numbered starting with Captain William Lumsdaine, who in India sired five children in a common-law marriage. Rumors among the family claimed Phoebe to have had an Indian princess among her immediate ancestors.

First Generation: **Captain William Lumsdaine** (1792-1830) was born in Canongate, Edinburgh, Scotland. He was an officer in the Bengal Army of the East India Company. His children with Phoebe Herrinjee Khanumal Dorrene were Louisa, Henry, Alexander, **William,** and John. Louisa was in school in England when her parents died of the cholera in Calcutta, India. The four boys embarked for Australia in 1836.

Second Generation: **William Lumsdaine** (1826-1902) married Mary Ann Hunt (1824-1916). He was born in Hissar, India and died in Gladesville, Australia. He was a minister in the Presbyterian Church for seven years and in the Church of England for 41 years. They had nine children: William Henry, **Edward Alexander**, Herbert Sinclair, Emmeline, Isobel Mason, Edwin Sandys, Percy Forrest, Mary Lillias, and Ethel Constance.

Third Generation: **Edward Alexander Lumsdaine** (1848-1943) married Florence Edith Halloran (1850-1884. They had six children: Victor Charles, Walter Halloran, Edward Leon, Allan, **Arthur Henry Vere**, and Allie. Edward Alexander was born in Sidney, Australia and was a solicitor.

Fourth Generation: **Arthur Henry Vere Lumsdaine** (1882-1962) married Mary Ellen Clifford (1881-1911); they had one son: **Clifford Vere** (1909-1996). Mary Ellen died of diabetes. Arthur Henry Vere married Gladys Ethel Strayer (1884-1961), with whom he had one son: Arthur Allen (1913-1989). Later, Arthur Henry Vere had two children with Gladys Ghys (1901-1994): Virginia Gladys Lumsdaine and Leon Sydney (Jack).

Fifth Generation: **Clifford Vere Lumsdaine** (1909-1996) married Ho Miao Ying (1910-1972) in Shanghai, and they had eleven children, nine living past infancy: Charles (Chuck), Yao-tim (Maria) **Edward,** George, Robert, Philip, Mildred (Milly), Dolly, and Joseph Albert.

Sixth Generation: **Edward Lumsdaine** married Monika Marlies Edith Amsler in Ventura, California, and God blessed them with four children: Andrew, Anne, Alfred and Arnold, as described in this book, which was written originally for their fourteen grandchildren (the seventh generation).

Appendix 2

Amsler Family Tree (Richterswiler Line)

This genealogical information is taken from a book compiled by Roger Amsler. He was born in Zürich (Switzerland) in 1940 and died of cancer in Boiling Springs, SC in 2008. He discovered that genealogical records were mainly kept in churches.

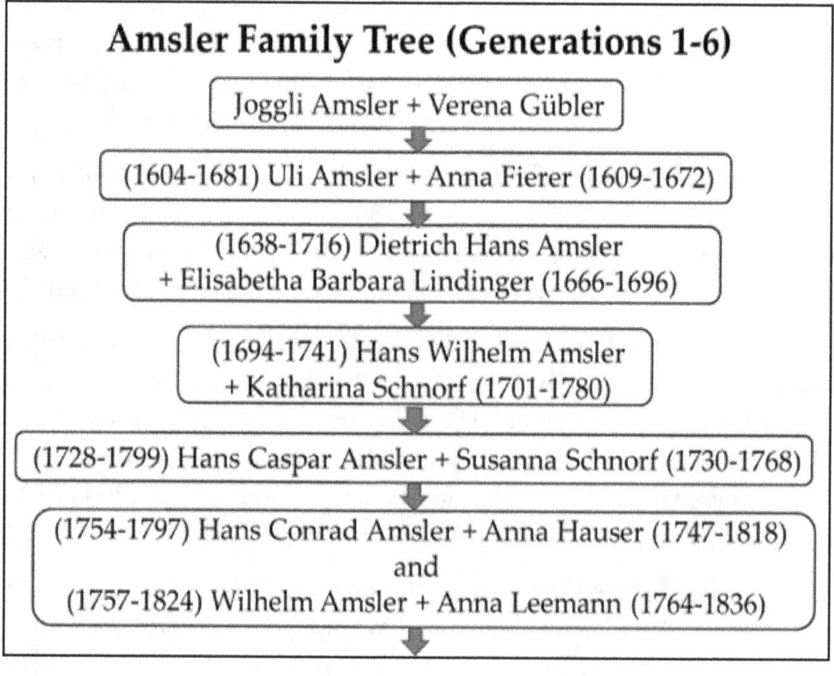

Amsler Family Tree (Generations 1-6)
Joggli Amsler + Verena Gübler
(1604-1681) Uli Amsler + Anna Fierer (1609-1672)
(1638-1716) Dietrich Hans Amsler
+ Elisabetha Barbara Lindinger (1666-1696)
(1694-1741) Hans Wilhelm Amsler
+ Katharina Schnorf (1701-1780)
(1728-1799) Hans Caspar Amsler + Susanna Schnorf (1730-1768)
(1754-1797) Hans Conrad Amsler + Anna Hauser (1747-1818)
and
(1757-1824) Wilhelm Amsler + Anna Leemann (1764-1836)

<u>**Seventh Generation:**</u> A sixth son, **Dietrich Hans Amsler**, was born in 1638 in Kempten. He was first an indentured tailor, then in 1688 became the innkeeper of "The Lion" in Meilen (on the shore of Lake Zürich). He was married six times (his first five wives died young). He married his fourth wife, Elisabetha Barbara Lindinger, in 1693; she died giving birth to her third child. Dietrich died in 1716 from a stroke.

Note: The inventor of the Amsler grid is a Swiss ophthalmologist, Marc Amsler. It is a tool to help identify vision problems like macular degeneration. He is not in Monika's genealogical line, to her disappointment, since she suffers from this condition.

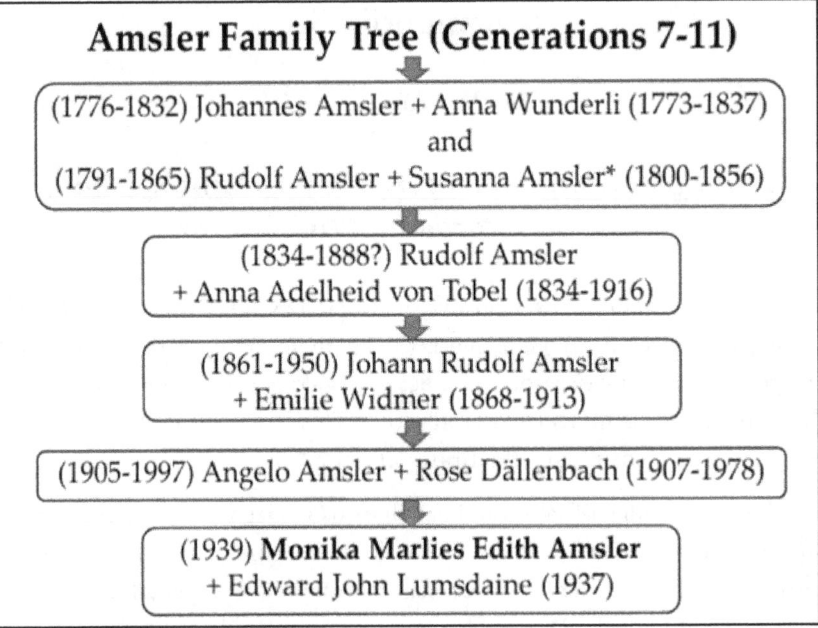

Amsler Family Tree (Generations 7-11)
(1776-1832) Johannes Amsler + Anna Wunderli (1773-1837)
and
(1791-1865) Rudolf Amsler + Susanna Amsler* (1800-1856)
(1834-1888?) Rudolf Amsler
+ Anna Adelheid von Tobel (1834-1916)
(1861-1950) Johann Rudolf Amsler
+ Emilie Widmer (1868-1913)
(1905-1997) Angelo Amsler + Rose Dällenbach (1907-1978)
(1939) Monika Marlies Edith Amsler
+ Edward John Lumsdaine (1937)

Eighth Generation: **Rudolf Amsler** was born in 1834 in Richterswil. He married Anna Adelheid von Tobel in Baden (Aargau). She was born in Richterswil in 1834. Rudolf was the innkeeper of the "Zum Raben" in Zürich-Aussersihl. Anna was a businesswoman; she owned a women's girdle factory and shop (in the Hotel Schwert am Weinplatz in Zürich). Around 1880, Rudolf disappeared in the US. The couple had two sons and five daughters. Anna died in 1916 at age 82.

Ninth Generation: Johann Rudolf Amsler was born in 1861 in Richterswil, but spent most of his life in Zürich. He was an insurance inspector. He married Emilie Widmer in 1890 (she was born in Killwangen-Aargau in 1868). They had eight children: Margrit, Ferdinand, Elly, Bertha, Milly, **Angelo**, Willi, and Julia. Johann Rudolf bought a house in Wiedikon where Emilie died in 1913 at age 46 from a heart attack. This makes Angelo the tenth and Monika the eleventh generation.

Appendix 3

The Bridge of Faith

Abridged from booklet by Troy L. Smith, ©1991, Portland, OR

The SAFE program focuses on five goals: (1) Lay the foundation which is Christ; (2) Develop a sound mind; (3) Learn to become responsible; (4) Improve your ability to resolve conflict and build good relationships; and (5) Strengthen your confidence in God's love. This last point is elaborated in a lesson called "Constructing the Bridge of Faith."

A strong bridge of faith can help all of us to become emotionally more stable and develop a sound mind. Since about 75% of our decisions are made in the subconscious mind, it is crucial that our mind is guided by a strong faith in God and His Word. However, a strong bridge of faith that will support us during difficult times does not just happen automatically—it must be constructed with care using the materials, wisdom, and guidance God has given us.

The bridge of faith has two supports that hold up each one of twelve planks. The two supports are: **God's Words** (focused on His promises) and **Prayer** (claiming the promises).

The planks are related to areas of our lives that require faith in God to see us safely through troubled times and difficulties, and each plank is focused on a special attribute of God. These attributes (each with Bible references) are listed below, followed by the study assignments.

1. ***God's Love:*** John 3:16; 1 John 3:1; Romans 5:8; 1 John 4:19.
2. ***God's Forgiveness:*** Acts 10:43; Psalms 32:5; Isaiah 44:22; 1 John 1:9; Ephesians 1:7.
3. ***God's Salvation:*** John 1:12; John 5:24; Romans 1:16; Ephesians 1:13; 1 John 5:12.
4. ***God's Provision:*** Isaiah 41:13; Psalms 34:10; Psalms 37:4; Psalms 84:11; Matthew 6:31-33.

5. ***God's Total Awareness:*** Proverbs 15:3; Psalms 147:5; Isaiah 41:10 and 58:9; Romans 8:28.

6. ***God's Protection:*** 11 Samuel 22:31; Romans 8:31; John 10: 27-28; 2 Chronicles 16:9.

7. ***God's Presence:*** Psalms 46:7,11; Deuteronomy 33:27; Psalms 23:4; John 14:17.

8. ***God's Goodness:*** 11 Chronicles 5:13; Deuteronomy 32:4; Psalms 100:4-5; Matthew 7:11.

9. ***God's Unlimited Power.*** Ephesians 1:19-20; 1 Chronicles 29:12; Luke 18:27; Romans 1:20.

10. ***God's Deliverance:*** Psalms 56:3-4; Psalms 34:6,17,19; Psalms 46:1; 1 Corinthians 10:13.

11. ***God's Guidance:*** Exodus 15:13; Psalms 32:8; Psalms 119:105; Proverbs 3:6; Luke 1:79.

12. ***God's Timing:*** Ecclesiastes 3:1, 11a; Psalms 27:14; James 1:4; Jeremiah 29:11-12; Lamentations 3:25-26; 2 Peter 3:8-9.

Assignment 1: Check out each plank by reading the corresponding verses. If you have trouble understanding the verses, use a Reference Bible and follow some of the links. Make sure you understand each of the attributes. You may also use a Concordance to find other verses relating to a particular attribute. The twelfth attribute has been hardest for me.

Assignment 2: Now examine your faith as it relates to each attribute. None of us have a strong faith in each area, but in order to grow, we need to identify our weak spots. In the first go-round, mark each attribute with V = very strong, S = strong, M = medium (so-so) or W = weak or wavering. Then do a second round and rank the attribute according to the strength of your faith, with 1 as the weakest and 12 as the strongest.

Assignment 3: It is easiest to change and work in one area at a time, starting with the one you have identified as the weakest. Now you need to make up a plan and find a partner who will help you by supporting you with prayer and monitoring your progress. You need to commit to have a regular time of prayer and to memorize one or more verses related to a particular attribute of God. Try to find people or stories who have developed and exhibited a strong faith in that area. How did they do it? Tip: See Romans 10:17. To keep your mind on Christ, also read a chapter a day in the Gospel of John.

Assignment 4: It may take several weeks to develop a new habit of discipline in prayer and Bible study. With your partner, review the verses you are memorizing. Once you are becoming more confident in one attribute of God, move on to the second weakest plank and repeat the process of prayer, study and memorizing key verses. Do not neglect thanksgiving for the progress that you are making!

Assignment 5: With your partner or your family, also frequently review and share your experiences with following Philippians 4:4-8. What prayers have been answered? How are you rejoicing? What good and true things are you thinking about? How have you overcome anxiety? For what are you especially thankful? What new insight about God have you learned this week? What new habit have you put into practice?

Assignment 6: If you are going through a period of depression or setbacks, here are three tips to encourage you.

(a) Read the story of Peter in the storm (Matthew 14:22-32). How can you set your eyes on Jesus? Think about how He has helped you in the past.

(b) Make a list of everything you are thankful for. See if you can get to 100 items where you are thankful without adding the caveat "but…". I want to share a secret: I have never been able to get to 100 because I felt a lot better about half-way there. The thing to remember is to start the list!

(c) Read the following, thanking God in prayer: Psalms 7, 28, 30, 35, 75, 100, 107, 118, and 136. Pick a verse that really is speaking to you and practice memorizing it within a week.

(d) Even if you are unable to keep up daily entries, try to maintain a journal and jot down the important concepts God is teaching you. These will with time turn into encouragements you can share with others about what God is doing in your life.

About the Authors

Edward Lumsdaine was born in Hong Kong and grew up in Shanghai, mostly during war times as told in his fascinating story *"Rotten Gambler Two Becomes a True American: A Boy's Journey of Surviving the Odds."* His mother was Chinese, his father an American merchant. After stints as a cabin boy and waiter on a Danish tramp steamer and four years in the US Air Force, he started his higher education on the GI Bill at Ventura Junior College. He soon met his wife-to-be, an exchange student from Switzerland. He then earned his BS ('63), MS ('64) and Ph.D ('66) degrees in mechanical engineering, all from New Mexico State University.

After working for the Boeing Company as research engineer, his love for teaching lured him to South Dakota State University, the University of Tennessee, and New Mexico State University. He advanced from Professor to administrative positions, starting as the Director of the New Mexico Solar Energy Institute and the Director of the Energy, Environment and Resources Center at the University of Tennessee. He then became Dean of Engineering at the University of Michigan-Dearborn, the University of Toledo, and Michigan Tech. On leave for two years, he worked as management consultant for the C3P program at Ford Motor Company. Also, he was a special professor of business at the University of Nottingham (UK), helping to set up the Institute for Enterprise and Innovation. He spent a sabbatical at Rose-Hulman Institute of Technology in Indiana and a year as distinguished visiting professor at the US Air Force Academy in Colorado Springs.

Many people urged him to jot down what to them were almost incredible experiences of survival. At a Blue Ridge Mountains Christian Writers Conference, he won third place for nonfiction for an early version of his childhood memoirs. Almost seven years later, he discovered an easy way to self-publish through Amazon/Kindle, starting with the story of his youth. This was quickly followed by the softcover edition printed by CreateSpace. Now fully retired, he plays harmonica and dulcimer with the "Tuesday Group that Plays on Monday" at the Museum of Appalachia in Clinton, TN.

Monika Lumsdaine came to the US from Switzerland in 1958 at the invitation of a Rotary family in Ventura, California, which enabled her to attend Ventura Junior College. The couple married at the end of their freshman year. Monika earned a BS degree in mathematics with highest honors from New Mexico State University in 1966. Some years later, she became involved in solar energy work through her husband. She founded her own consulting company and designed mainly passive solar homes for private clients. One design won a national award from HUD/DOE.

Edward and Monika have raised four children and built two passive solar homes for their family. They have co-authored textbooks in engineering design and entrepreneurship that focus on creative problem solving. Together, they have taught workshops all over the US and overseas. Monika became certified in the administration and interpretation of the Herrmann Brain Dominance Instrument (HBDI) and has conducted longitudinal research into the thinking preferences of engineering students. As Management Consultant for Corporate Behavior, she conducted team-building workshops in industry, hospitals, and universities (for students, faculty and staff).

Since her retirement, her hobby is wildflower photography, especially during springtime in the Great Smoky Mountains. Besides spending as much time as possible with grandchildren, her primary task starting in 2015 was helping Edward with writing, editing, and publishing the story of his youth, followed by their complex love story, where she added much new text about her childhood and their enduring partnership. Especially, she elaborates how God's providence and never-ending love can be discerned throughout the course of their lives. She feels honored that the American Legion Auxiliary of Post 2 in Knoxville has elected her as Chaplain for the current year.

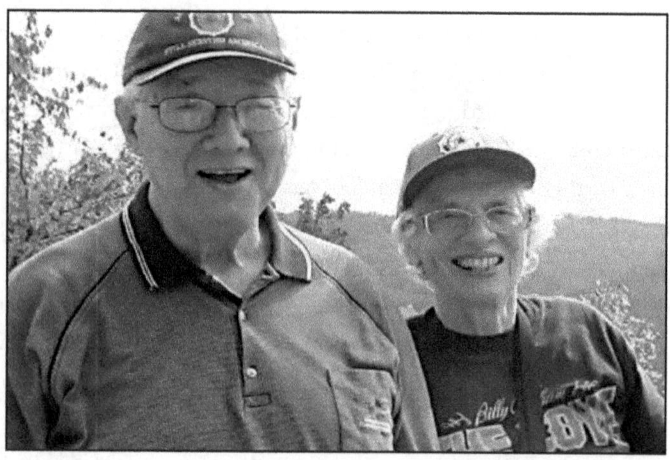

Acknowledgments

I (Monika) want to start our acknowledgments with a special remembrance of the family who was instrumental in my coming to America, thereby completely changing the direction of our lives. I owe a debt of gratitude to Arthur Langford, a member and past president of the Ventura Rotary Club, who sponsored my first year in America as a college student. He, with his wife Esther and sparkling daughter, Artie, provided a truly loving home for me! Sadly, there is no way I can repay this debt since Art passed away in 1982, Esther in 1995, and Artie in 2007. Without them, our love story would not have happened. I thank God for giving me the gift of this special family as an introduction to my new country! This photo of Art and Esther during our last visit to Rancho Arnaz in 1969 includes our three older children and Esther's brown poodle.

From our heart we want to thank our daughter Anne and her son Edward for their early help and proof-reading to make the manuscript of this book more readable. Sarah Lumsdaine and Bethany Lumsdaine have also done a great job in professional editing from the viewpoint of the next two generations. We are grateful!

We appreciate Corrine Sahlberg's tip for conceptualizing a version of our story for our grandchildren. Corrine and her husband Elmer served as C&MA missionaries to Thailand from 1950 to 1985. She died at age 96 in 2018. Others that have given us early feedback are Pastor Vern Holstad and Bible-teacher Betty King, both now home with our Heavenly Father.

We also value the readers of *Rotten Gambler Two Becomes a True American: A Boy's Journey of Survival,* who said they can hardly wait for the sequel of

Edward's life story (which now includes Monika as co-author). We thank Brigit König for her review and comments from a Swiss perspective, as well as Bill Raney, Dolores Moore and Bob Moore for their painstaking proof-reading of early chapters of *Chopsticks and Chocolate.* "Saints Alive" Sunday school class, thanks so much for your prayers and your encouragement!

About the time I completed the draft of Volume 2, the sequel to *Chopsticks and Chocolate,* I noticed the Kharis Publishing posting. For a time, they were accepting queries. I emailed in a brief summary of Volume 1 and was surprised they wanted us to submit a formal proposal. It had many questions about the book, its purpose, and what readers we were hoping to attract. What impressed us most was the Christian emphasis of this company, and how their chief aim was to honor God. Then they asked for the complete manuscript. Our book had over eighty photos, so this presented a problem for the MS Word format, though not for the pdf. I did send in both documents, but for some reason, the Word format went astray. In the meantime, we realized Volume 2 would be too difficult to do. Therefore, in the next few weeks, I condensed the contents down to a Postscript focused on Edward's spiritual journey of redemption from gambling addiction. When we received an inquiry from Kharis about the original manuscript, we amended the formal proposal, which now included the Postscript and God's larger purpose of reaching readers from teenagers to seniors with His story of how He worked (often behind the scenes) in our lives. This could be a help to others on how to find Him and be saved by His love for them.

In response to the updated manuscript and sooner than expected, we received Kharis's willingness to sign a contract and publish our book. We tried to meet their requirements and submitted five testimonials, as well as a video about us and our book (which was much more difficult to do for us than we expected, and for which we are grateful to Stephen Ballast, Cedar Springs Presbyterian Church, for producing it after days of preparation on our side (and putting it together on his side).

All along, my main contact person was James Clement, the Project Coordinator. We very much appreciate his patience with us, when we had to ask for extra time or other extensions to meet their requirements, or when there were misunderstandings about the editing process and formatting (a very tedious undertaking). Then we encountered some obstacles, such as a tree falling on our car from tropical storm Fred when we were out of town.

I was very impressed with the work of Emma Grace, the Cover Designer. Her final concept, which included a background based on the pattern of a Lake Superior agate, was simply brilliant, and I feel the cover really entices potential readers to take a closer look into the book.

Simultaneously, Victoria Trutie was editing the manuscript. Once I received this annotated document, I incorporated all the changes into my Word manuscript. Thank you for an incredible job, including punctuation and deleting superfluous spacing!

Next came Interior Design and Alignment by James Clement and Rufus Philips. I learned that Kharis required Garamond size 11 font with other formatting changes (where I had a choice as to paragraphing and line spacing). I tried out various formats, and then began to convert my Word version to meet these requirements. The largest challenge was keeping a correct placement for the photos within the text. To achieve a nice layout for each page, I had to change some of the text (many of these were minor, but there were some additional paragraphs, and the size of some photos had to be altered). When I mentioned the format specs I was using, James Clement informed me that they would do the interior formatting, but then asked for what I had already done in a pdf. Because I had previous experience in formatting from doing books many years ago, I was complimented for my work. But it was nice "to let go" and let the professionals do this work. Subsequently, I had a chance for another review and make further changes needed to eliminate white space, now including over 90 photos.

Rufus Philips will be in charge of Media and Marketing, and we are looking forward to that phase of which we know very little. The Chief Director/Chief Editorial Officer is Prof. Francis E. Umesini. Our gratitude extends to everyone who is involved in getting our book published successfully; we never had this kind of view behind the scenes nor any idea of the entire process and work involved with a team who wants to honor our Savior Jesus Christ. God bless you all!

Above all, our hearts overflow with gratitude to our God who has patiently watched over us, protected us, brought us together, drew us to Him, and blessed us with four precious children and fourteen grandchildren. This book is truly a love story, not only of two people from very different parts of the world and cultures, but of God's never-ending love, faithfulness and purpose in the journey of our family's life!

Source Materials

1. *The Grandparent Book for Arnold Lumsdaine* by Yao-tim Lumsdaine-Allen, 20 December 1995.
2. *Photo Album of Angelo and Rose Amsler,* compiled and copied digitally by their granddaughter Anne Lumsdaine, 15 December 2009.
3. Ring Binder with a collection of letters written by Monika Amsler to her parents after she traveled to the US on a student visa, then continued as Monika Lumsdaine, ending with Letter #327 (Dec 14, 1968) and a few later photos. This Binder was compiled by Anne Lumsdaine for her brothers.
4. Geoffrey Lumsdaine, *Transition to the Colony: An Australian Family,* 1997 edition and related website, www.lumsdaine.org.au/Home.html (accessed April 11, 2016 to download the portrait of Captain William and Phoebe). We were sent Lumsdaine genealogical charts by Joseph A. Lumsdaine in 1997, with permission to discuss and distribute freely by Geoffrey Lumsdaine.
5. *Meine Heimat: Ein Buch für Schweizer im Ausland (1942).* A gift from the Gemeinde Kriens to Monika Amsler on her twentieth birthday. Pages 98-105 discuss the first three years of World War II and how they affected Switzerland (Author: Dr. Hans Rudolf Schmid, Thalwil).
6. Joshua Rothman, "The Meaning of Culture," *The New Yorker,* 26 Dec 2014 (accessed online).
7. Edward Lumsdaine, *Rotten Gambler Two Becomes a True American,* ©2017, available from amazon.com.
8. Interview with Edward's cousin Ho Siu Hwa, Hong Kong, in May 2019.
9. Joseph Albert Lumsdaine, INDOMITABLE, received in February 2021 (Clifford and Ho Miao Ying's love story).

Index of Photos